The Gen X Series

IMO NSO NCO IEO

International Mathematics Olympiad | National Science Olympiad | National Cyber Olympiad | International English Olympiad

OLYMPIAD SAMPLE PAPERS 9

Useful for Olympiads Conducted at School, National & International Levels

Compiled By
Editorial Board

Strictly According to the Latest Syllabus of Olympiad

V&S PUBLISHERS

Published by:

V&S PUBLISHERS

F-2/16, Ansari road, Daryaganj, New Delhi-110002
☎ 23240026, 23240027 • *Fax:* 011-23240028
Email: info@vspublishers.com • *Website:* www.vspublishers.com

Regional Office : Hyderabad
5-1-707/1, Brij Bhawan (Beside Central Bank of India Lane)
Bank Street, Koti, Hyderabad - 500 095
☎ 040-24737290
E-mail: vspublishershyd@gmail.com

Branch Office : Mumbai
Jaywant Industrial Estate, 1st Floor–108, Tardeo Road
Opposite Sobo Central Mall, Mumbai – 400 034
☎ 022-23510736
E-mail: vspublishersmum@gmail.com

ISBN 978-93-579423-4-8
New Edition

DISCLAIMER

Publisher's Note

The current decade has firmly established V&S Publishers as one of the Leading Publishers of General Trade Mass Appeal Books across popular genres along with Academic Books for School Children. Having been in publishing trade for over 40 years, we understand the need of the hour when it comes to Books. After successfully publishing around 600 titles in the last decade and establishing a pan India network of booksellers & distributors including ecommerce platforms – Amazon, Flipkart etc; we determined after a nation-wide market research in tier 1, 2 and 3 cities that preparatory materials for status-acquiring OLYMPIAD BOOKS is the need of the hour.

And in true spirit, the Olympiad books on Science, Maths, English and Cyber published for classes 1 to 10 was picked by students off the shelf in no time. It acquired the 'Bestseller' image. Encouraged by this huge acceptability of our Olympiad Series among parents, students and booksellers alike, we at V&S Publishers decided to take PREPARATION to the next level by bringing out another handholding masterpiece – Olympiad Sample Papers.

These Sample Papers are the virtual replicas of the actual exam papers.

Yes! These Sample Papers are the virtual replicas of the actual exam papers. Inclusion of two sets each for Science, Maths, English and Cyber subjects from classes 1 to 10 in respective books are believed to be adequate to prepare students mentally for 'live exam conditions.' Anything else would have been 'under-preparation' or over-preparation'

You will hardly be able to differentiate the Sample Papers from the Actual Exam Papers. All this has been made possible by the people who have been in their respective fields for years – coaching and guiding students to succeed in this vital exam.

P.S. While every care has been taken to ensure correctness of content, if you come across any error, howsoever minor, anywhere in the book, do not hesitate to discuss with your teachers while pointing that out to us in no uncertain terms.

We wish you All the Best!

Contents

INTERNATIONAL MATHEMATICS OLYMPIAD (IMO)

Mock Test Paper 1

I M O

INTERNATIONAL MATHEMATICS OLYMPIAD

Total Questions : 50 Time : 1 Hour

PATTERN AND MARKING SCHEME				
Section	**(1) Logical Reasoning**	**(2) Mathematical Reasoning**	**(3) Everyday Mathematics**	**(4) Achievers Section**
No. of Questions	15	20	10	5
Marks per Questions	1	1	1	3

SYLLABUS

Section – 1: Verbal and Non-Verbal Reasoning.

Section – 2: Number Systems, Polynomials, Coordinate Geometry, Linear Equations in Two Variables, Introduction to Euclid's Geometry, Lines and Angles, Triangles, Quadrilaterals, Areas of Parallelograms and Triangles, Circles, Constructions, Heron's Formula, Surface Areas and Volumes, Statistics, Probability.

Section – 3: The syllabus of this section will be based on the syllabus of Mathematical Reasoning and Quantitative Aptitude.

Section – 4: Higher Order Thinking Questions – Syllabus as per Section – 2.

LOGICAL REASONING

1. If the first and the last letters of the word IMPOSSIBLE are interchanged, the second and second last letters are interchanged and so on. Which one out of the following will be the fourth letter from the right end?
   (A) K (B) M
   (C) O (D) None of these

2. If 'a' stands for '×', 'b' stands for '÷', 'c' stands for '–' and 'd' stands for '+', then what will be the value of the expression (10 a 3) b (14 c 4) d (19 d 9) ?
   (A) 21 (B) 49
   (C) 13 (D) 31

3. P is shorter than Q who is taller than S. R is shorter than P. R is not as tall as 5.Q is not as tall as T. The shortest one and the tallest one respectively are __________.
   (A) P, E (B) R, P
   (C) R, T (D) Q, R

4. In a certain code language, TRIPPLE is written as SQHOOKD. How is DISPOSE written in that code ?
   (A) ESJKFTP
   (B) DSPABHI
   (C) CHRONRD
   (D) None of these

5. Select the figure from the options which can be formed from the pieces given in Figure (X).

Fig. (X)

(A) 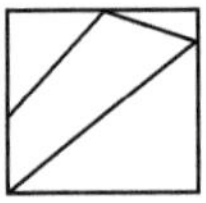 (B) 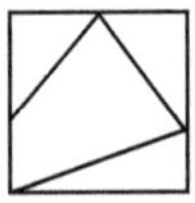

(C) 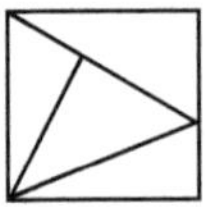 (D) 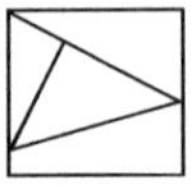

6. Choose an alternative figure which has the same conditions of regions in which the dot(s) must be placed as in the given Fig. (X).

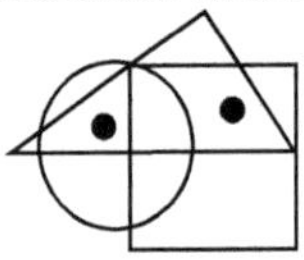

Fig. (X)

(A) 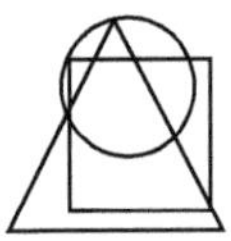 (B) 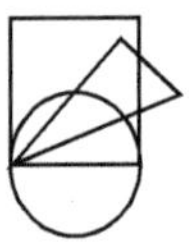

(C)  (D) 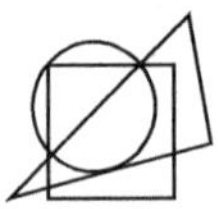

7. Two positions of a brick are shown below. When the number 6 will be on the top, then which number will be at the bottom?

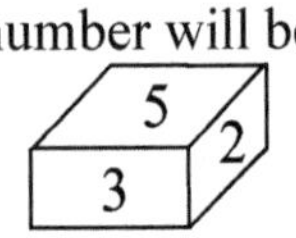

(i)

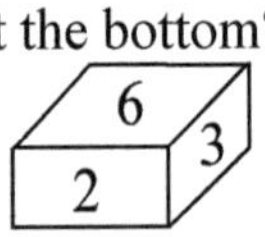

(ii)

(A) 1 (B) 5
(C) 2 (D) 4

8. Select a figure from the options that would show the unfolded form of Fig. (X).

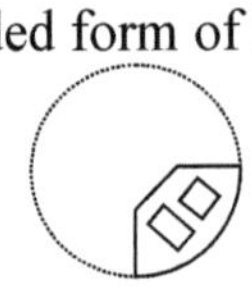

Fig. (X)

(A) 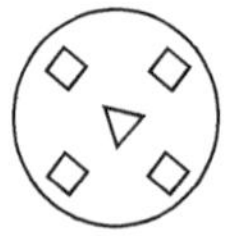 (B) 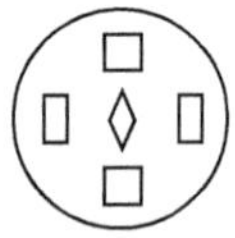

(C)  (D) 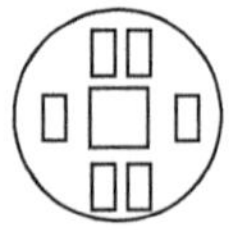

9. Identify the figure that will complete the figure matrix.

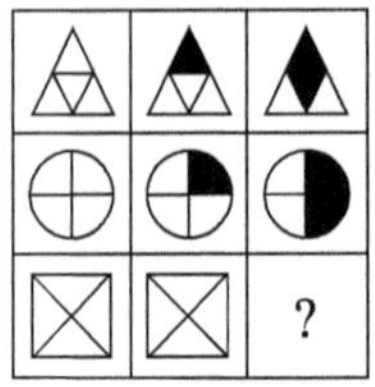

(A)  (B) 

(C) 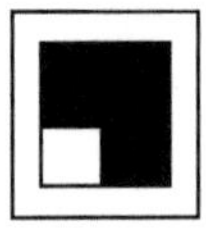 (D) 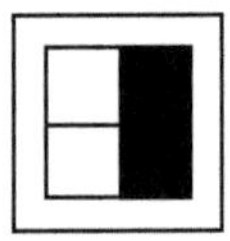

10. Select the figure from the options given below in which the given fig. (X) is embedded as one of its part.

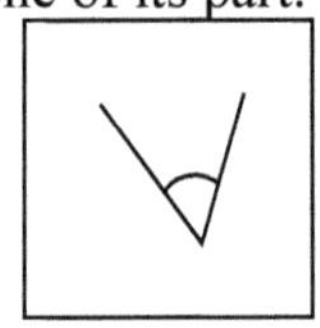

Fig. (X)

(A)  (B) 

(C) 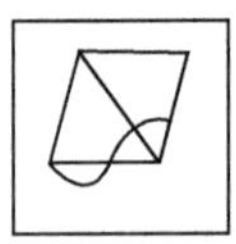 (D) 

11. Choose the mirror image of the given figure (X) from the given alternatives.

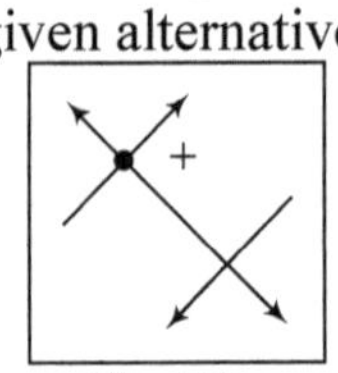

Fig. (X)

(A) 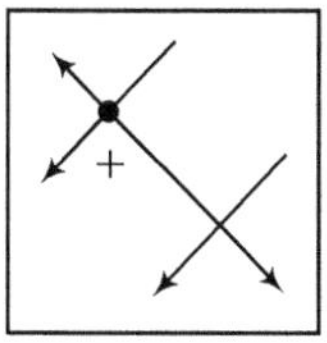 (B) 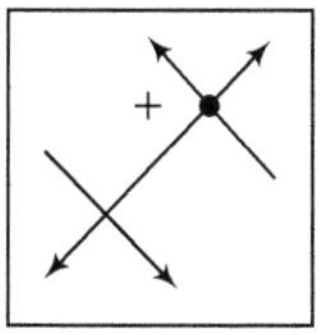

(C) 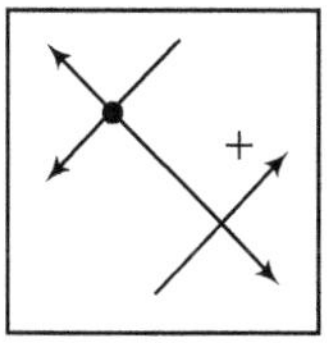 (D) 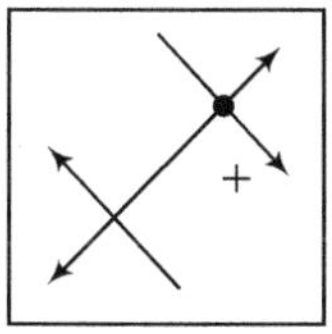

12. How many triangles does the given figure consist of ?

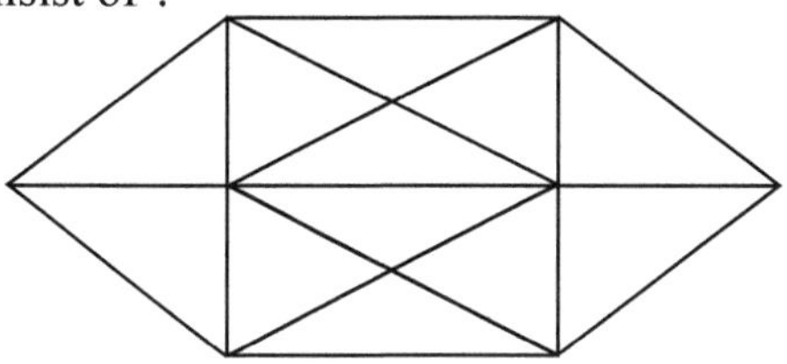

(A) 24 (B) 12
(C) 28 (D) None of these

13. Choose the figure from the given options that will complete the series.

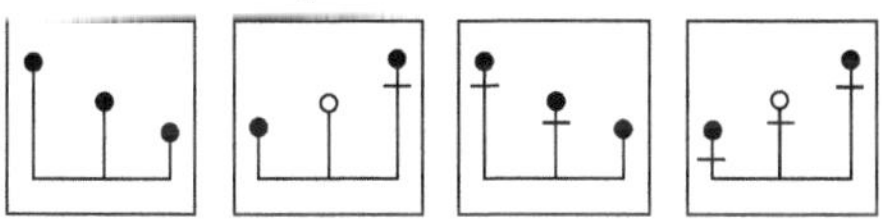
?

(A) 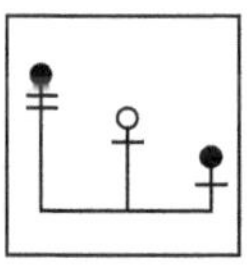 (B) 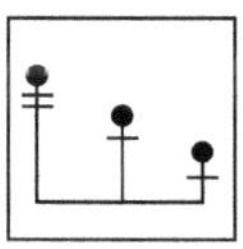

(C) 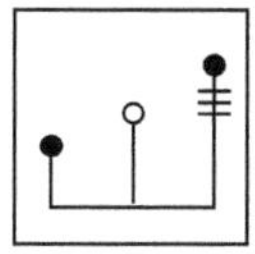 (D) 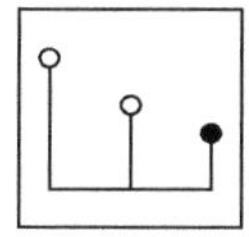

14. Complete the analogy.

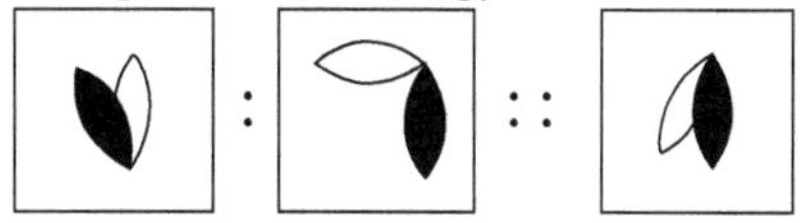
?

(A)  (B) 

(C) 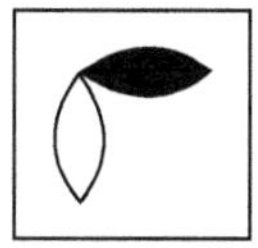 (D) 

15. Find the figure which is different from the others.

(A) 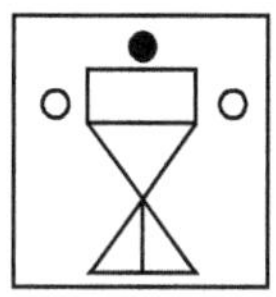 (B) 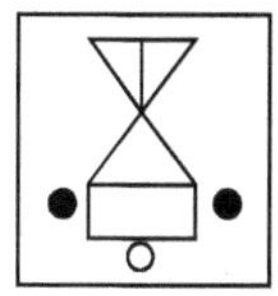

(C) 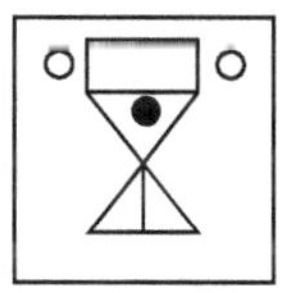 (D) 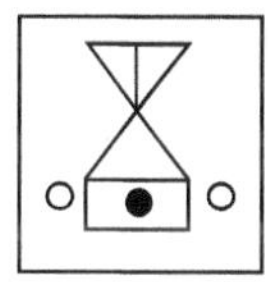

MATHEMATICAL REASONING

16. A bag contains 4 white, 5 red and 6 black balls. One ball is drawn at random. What is the probability that the ball drawn is neither black nor white?

(A) 1/3 (B) 4/15
(C) 3/4 (D) None of these

17. AD is the diameter of a circle and AB is a chord. If AD = 34 cm, AB = 30 cm, then find the distance of AB from the centre of the circle.

(A) 12 cm (B) 32 cm
(C) 8 cm (D) 25 cm

18. In the given figure, ABCD is a parallelogram. AE perpendicular on DC and CF perpendicular on AD. If AD = 12 cm, AE = 8 cm and CF = 10 cm, then find CD.

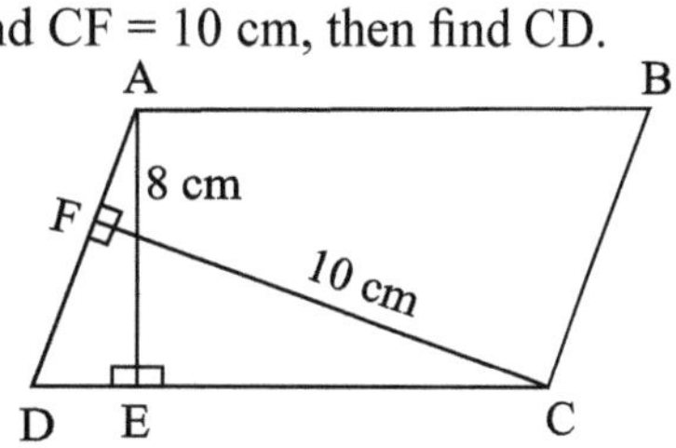

(A) 24 cm (B) 22 cm
(C) 15 cm (D) 12 cm

19. In a quadrilateral ABCD, the line segments bisecting $\angle C$ and $\angle D$ meet at E. Then find the sum of $\angle A$ and $\angle B$.

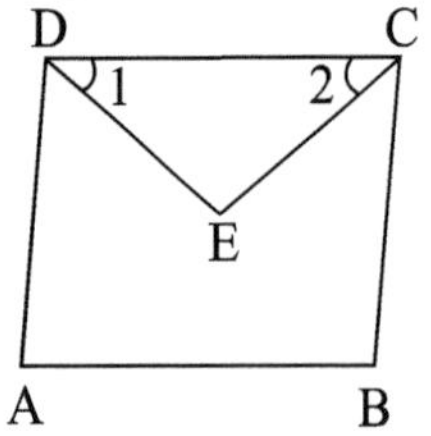

(A) $\angle CED$ (B) $1/2 \angle CED$
(C) $2 \angle CED$ (D) None of these

20. Find the values of m and n when $(x^3 - 2x^2 + mx - q)$ is divided by $(x^2 - 2x - 3)$ and the remainder is $(x - 6)$.
(A) –2, –6 (B) 2, –6
(C) –2, 6 (D) 2, 6

21. In the adjoining figure, find the area of the shaded portion.

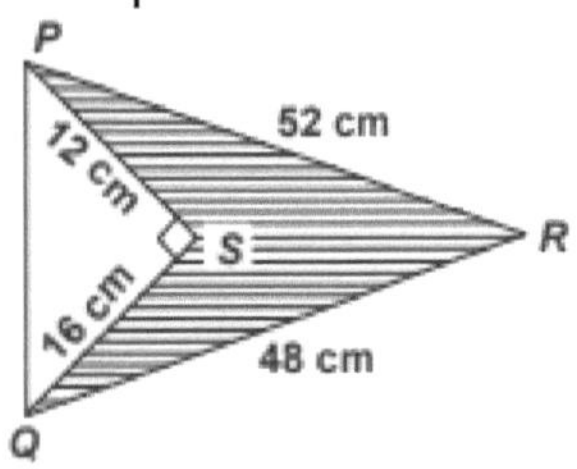

(A) 98 cm^2 (B) 480 cm^2
(C) 384 cm^2 (D) None of these

22. If $2^{x-3} . 3^{2x-8} = 36$, then find the value of x.
(A) 2 (B) 5
(C) 3 (D) 1

23. In the given figure, find the value of x.

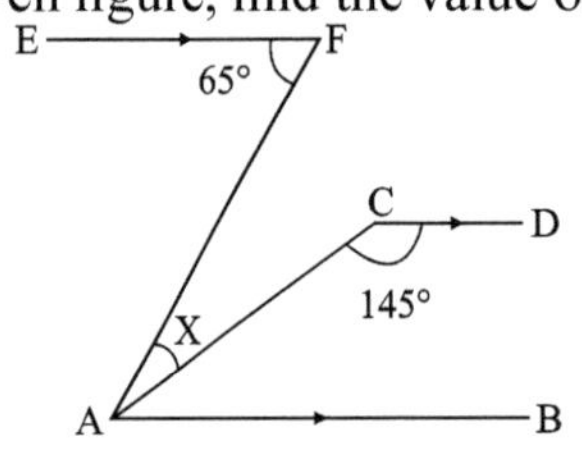

(A) 30° (B) 10°
(C) 40° (D) 20°

24. Simplify $\sqrt[4]{(81)^{-2}}$
(A) 1/9 (B) 1/3
(C) 9 (D) 1/81

25. A rhombus-shaped sheet with perimeter 40 cm and one diagonal 12 cm, is painted on both sides at the rate of ₹ 5 per cm^2. Find the cost of painting.
(A) ₹ 980 (B) ₹ 1020
(C) ₹ 960 (D) ₹ 880

26. The radii of two cylinders are in the ratio 2 : 3 and their heights are in the ratio of 5 : 3. Find the ratio of their volumes.
(A) 10 : 27 (B) 20 : 27
(C) 17 : 27 (D) 20 : 37

27. Find the value of 1/3 of 15^{27}.
(A) 5^{27} (B) 5×15^{26}
(C) 15^9 (D) 5×3^9

28. Find the co-ordinates of point R if PQRS forms a rectangle from the diagram given below.

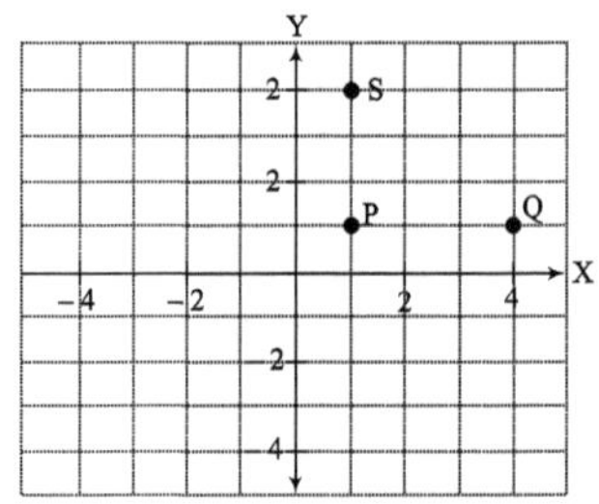

(A) (2, 6) (B) (0, 0)
(C) (4, 4) (D) (6, 4)

29. If (2, 0) is a solution of the linear equation $2x + 3y = k$, then find the value of k.
(A) 1 (B) 6
(C) 4 (D) None of these

30. Find the value of x.

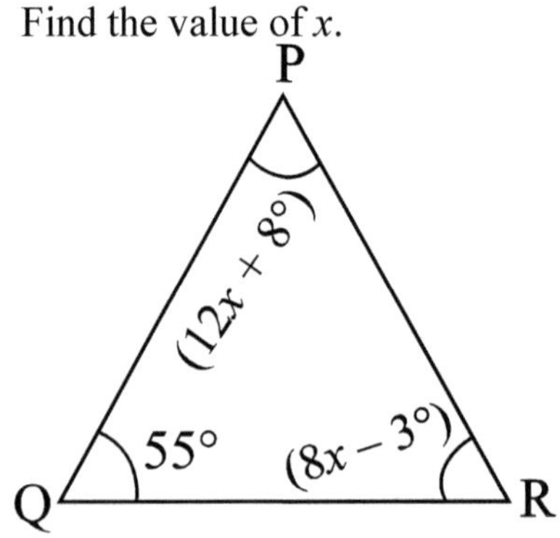

(A) 4° (B) 6°
(C) 8° (D) None of these

31. In the given figure PR = OS then which of the following axioms shows that PQ = RS ?

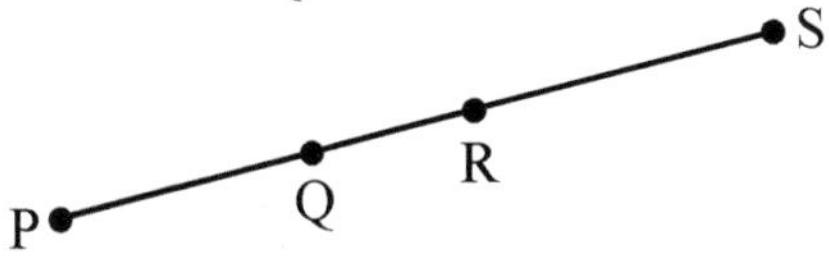

(A) The whole is greater than the part.
(B) If equals are subtracted from equals, the remainders are equal.
(C) Things which are equal to the same things are equal to one another.
(D) None of these

32. In the given figure, if AE = AD and BD = CE, then ________.

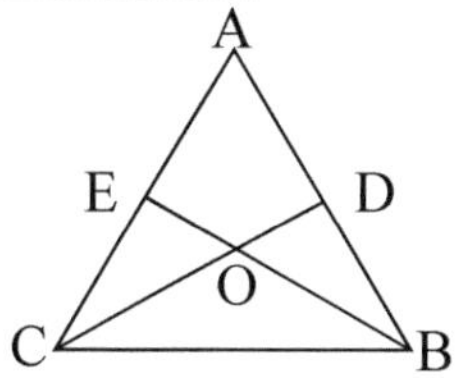

(A) BD = CD (B) $\Delta BEC \cong \Delta BDC$
(C) $\triangle AEB \cong \Delta ADC$ (D) None of these

33. A metal sheet 27 cm long, 8 cm broad and 1 cm thick is melted into a cube. Find the difference between surface areas of two solids.
(A) 306 cm^2 (B) 516 cm^2
(C) 286 cm^2 (D) None of these

34. A field is in the shape of a trapezium whose parallel sides are 25 m and 10 m. The non-parallel sides are 14 m and 13 m. Find the area of the field.
(A) 146 cm^2 (B) 196 cm^2
(C) 286 cm^2 (D) 89 cm^2

35. The mean of 100 observations is 50. If one of the observations which was 50 is replaced by 150, find the resulting mean.
(A) 50.5 (B) 51
(C) 51.5 (D) 52

EVERYDAY MATHEMATICS

36. Akash scored 63 marks in Economics, 57 in Accounts, 82 in Mathematics, 55 in Business studies and x in English. If the average he scored is 60, find the average of best four of the them.
(A) 64.25 (B) 85.15
(C) 24.25 (D) 80.75

37. Find the cost of laying grass in a triangular field of sides 50 m, 65 m and 65 m at the rate of ₹ 7 per m^2 .
(A) ₹ 5500 (B) ₹ 17800
(C) ₹ 8500 (D) ₹ 10500

38. The perimeter of a rectangular field is 80 m. If the length of the field is decreased by 2 m and its breadth is increased by 2 m, the area of the field is increased by 16 m^2. Find the length and breadth of the rectangular field.
(A) 25 m, 15 m
(B) 21 m, 10 m
(C) 30 m, 19 m
(D) None of these

39. If the radius of a circle is decreased by 50%, find the percentage decrease in its area.
(A) 40% (B) 75%
(C) 50% (D) 20%

40. The cost of a notebook is twice the cost of a pen. If the cost of a notebook is – x and that of a pen is – y, then express it in a linear equation in two variables to represent the given condition.
(A) $x - 2y = 0$ (B) $x + 2y = 0$
(C) $2x - y=0$ (D) $2x + y = 0$

41. An article is sold at a certain price. By selling it at 2/3 of that price one loses 10%. Find the gain percent at original price
(A) 15% (B) 35%
(C) 25% (D) 30%

42. The perimeter of a field in the form of an equilateral triangle is 36 cm, then find its area.

(A) $28\sqrt{3}$ cm^2 (B) $36\sqrt{3}$ cm^2

(C) $8\sqrt{3}$ cm^2 (D) $12\sqrt{3}$ cm^2

43. Shivani has ₹ $(x^3 - 3x^2 + 4x + 50)$. She wants to buy chocolates each of cost ₹ $(x - 3)$. After buying maximum number of chocolates with her money, how much money is left with her?

(A) ₹ 10 (B) ₹ 38

(C) ₹ 56 (D) ₹ 62

44. In a cricket match, Sehwag hits the boundary 15 times out of 20 balls played by him. Find the probability that the boundary is not hit by the Sehwag.

(A) 3/2 (B) 5/8

(C) 1/4 (D) 4/3

45. How many bricks, each measuring 25 cm × 11.25 cm × 6 cm, will be needed to build a wall measuring 8 m × 6 m × 22.5 cm?

(A) 3200 (B) 8000

(C) 9200 (D) 6400

ACHIEVERS SECTION

46. If the sides BA and DC of quadrilateral ABCD are produced as shown in the given figure, then select the correct option.

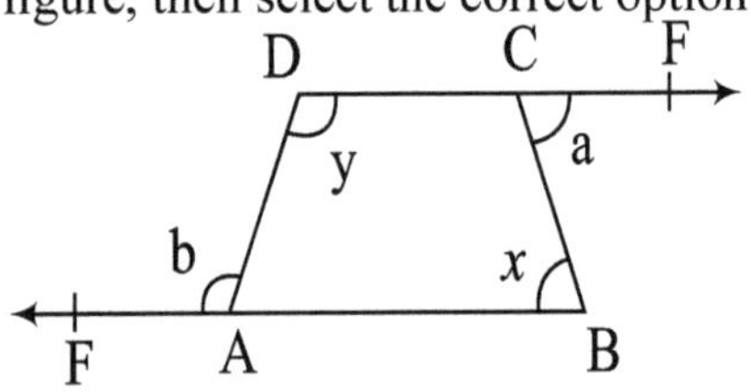

(A) $2(x + y) = a + b$

(B) $x - y = a - b$

(C) $x + y = a + b$

(D) None of these

47. Find the area of quadrilateral ABCD in which AB = 9 cm, BC = 40 cm, CD = 28 cm, DA = 15 cm and ∠ABC = 90°.

(A) 150 cm^2

(B) 306 cm^2

(C) 180 cm^2

(D) 450 cm^2

48. In the given figure, AOB is the diameter of a circle and CD || AB. If ∠BAD = 30°, then find ∠CAD.

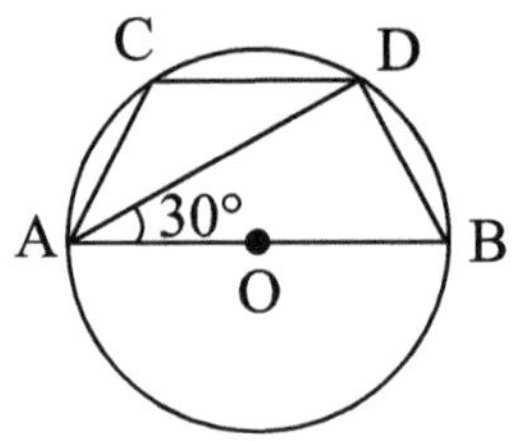

(A) 80° (B) 30°

(C) 50° (D) None of these

49. A cylindrical tub of radius 12 cm contains water to a depth of 20 cm. A spherical iron ball is dropped into the tub and thus the level of the water is raised by 6.75 cm. What is the radius of the sphere?

(A) 4 cm (B) 15 cm

(C) 9 cm (D) 12 cm

50. ABCD is a parallelogram in which BC is produced to E such that CE = BC. AE intersects CD at F. If area of ΔDFA is 3 cm^2, then find the area of parallelogram ABCD.

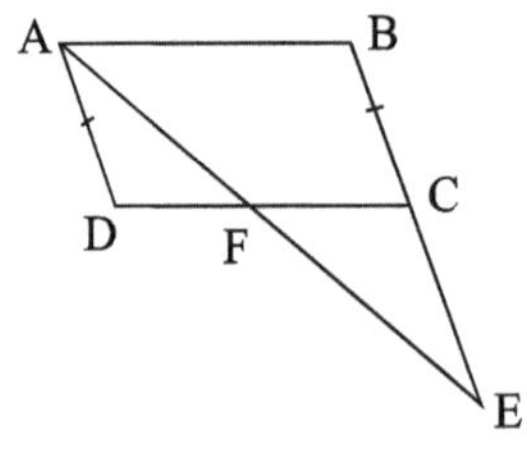

(A) 12 cm^2 (B) 22 cm^2

(C) 10 cm^2 (D) 28 cm^2

Mock Test Paper 2

Total Questions : 50 Time : 1 Hour

I M O

INTERNATIONAL MATHEMATICS OLYMPIAD

PATTERN AND MARKING SCHEME				
Section	**(1) Logical Reasoning**	**(2) Mathematical Reasoning**	**(3) Everyday Mathematics**	**(3) Achievers Section**
No. of Questions	15	20	10	5
Marks per Questions	1	1	1	3

SYLLABUS

Section – 1: Verbal and Non-Verbal Reasoning.

Section – 2: Number Systems, Polynomials, Coordinate Geometry, Linear Equations in Two Variables, Introduction to Euclid's Geometry, Lines and Angles, Triangles, Quadrilaterals, Areas of Parallelograms and Triangles, Circles, Constructions, Heron's Formula, Surface Areas and Volumes, Statistics, Probability.

Section – 3: The syllabus of this section will be based on the syllabus of Mathematical Reasoning and Quantitative Aptitude.

Section – 4: Higher Order Thinking Questions – Syllabus as per Section – 2.

LOGICAL REASONING

1. Choose the odd one out.
   (A) (10 – 1000) (B) (2 – 8)
   (C) (5 – 125) (D) (7 – 341)

2. Triangle represents the married persons Circle represents unemployed, Square represents women, Rectangle represents non-vegetarians

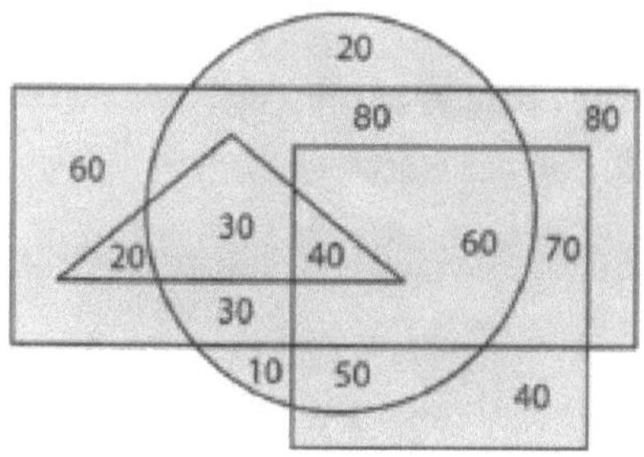

   Find the number of married women who are unemployed and non-vegetarians.
   (A) 15 (B) 40
   (C) 25 (D) None of these

3. Kalpana drove her car for 4 km in East. She then turned in South-West and drove for 5 km. She then turned in East and drove for 4 km. She again turned in North-West and drove for 5 km. What was the shortest distance between Kalpana's initial and final positions?
   (A) 12 km (B) 7.5 km
   (C) 4 km (D) None of these

4. If A + B means A is the mother of B; A – B means A is the brother B; A % B means A is the father of B and A × B means A is the sister of B, which of the following shows that P is the maternal uncle of Q?
   (A) Q – N + M × P
   (B) P + S × N – Q
   (C) P – M + N × Q
   (D) Q – S % P

5. In a particular language, 'body' means 'bone', 'bone' means 'head', 'head' means 'knee', 'knee'means 'elbow' and 'elbow' means 'feet'. On which part of body does a man wear hat?

(A) elbow (B) head
(C) knee (D) feet

6. Select one figure from given options which fits exactly into the given Fig. (X) in order to form a complete square.

Fig. (X)

(A)  (B) 

(C)  (D) 

7. Count the number of cubes in the figure given below.

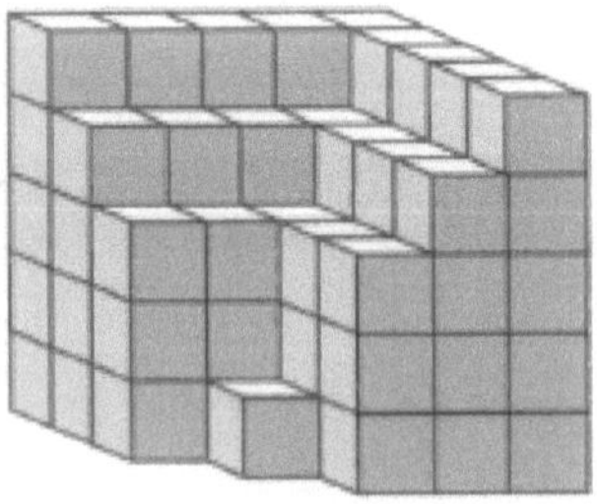

(A) 80 (B) 89
(C) 120 (D) 90

8. Find the figure that will complete the figure matrix.

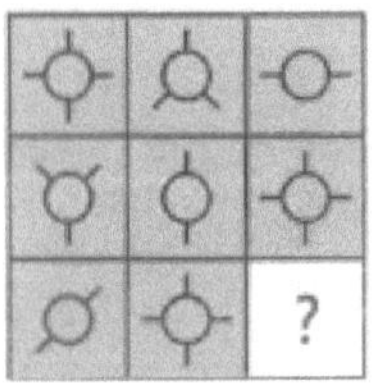

(A)  (B) 

(C)  (D) 

9. Which of the figures from the given alternative would show the unfolded form of fig (X)?

Fig. (X)

(A) 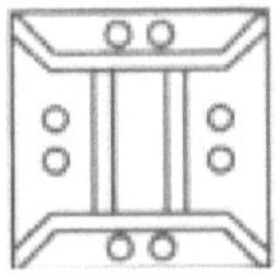 (B) 

(C) 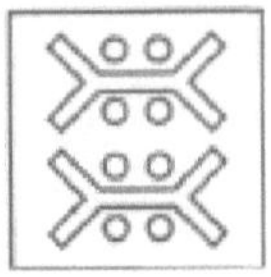 (D) 

10. Select the figure from the options given below in which the given fig. (X) is embedded as one of its part.

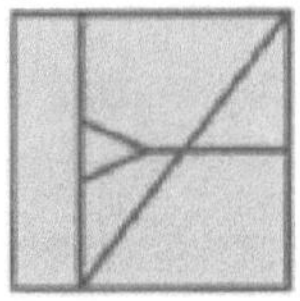

Fig. (X)

(A) 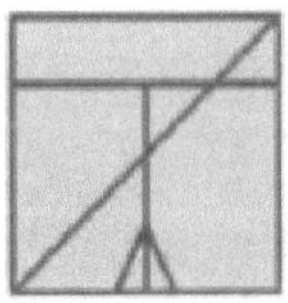 (B) 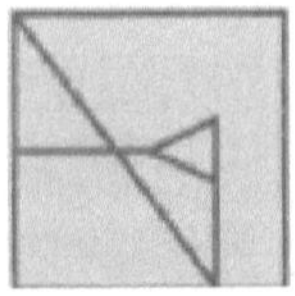

(C) 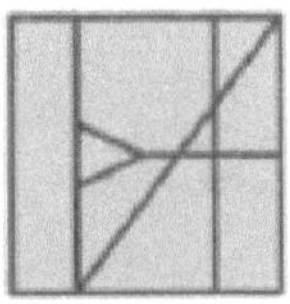 (D) 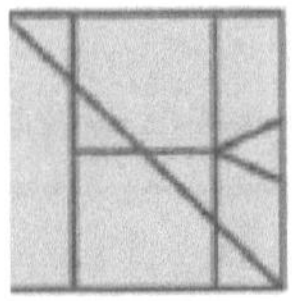

11. Select suitable mirror image of the given figure if the mirror is placed along the line MN.

(A)  (B) 

(C)  (D) 

12. Select correct water image of the given figure (X).

Fig. (X)

(A)  (B) 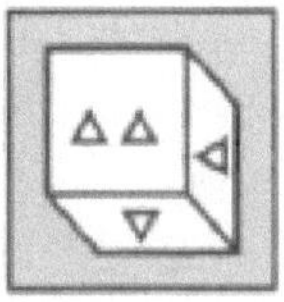

(C)  (D) 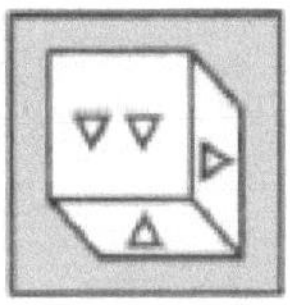

13. How many rectangles are there in the adjoining figure?

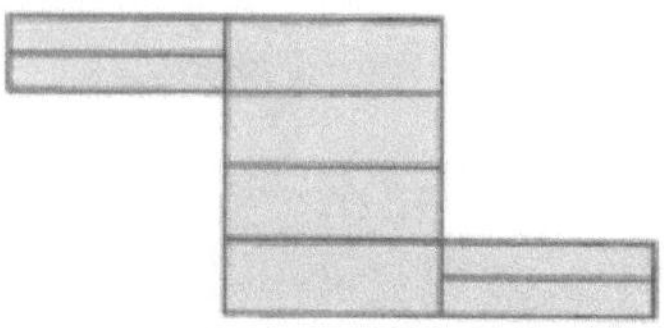

(A) 6 (B) 18
(C) 22 (D) 10

14. Select a figure from the given options that will complete the second pair as the first one.

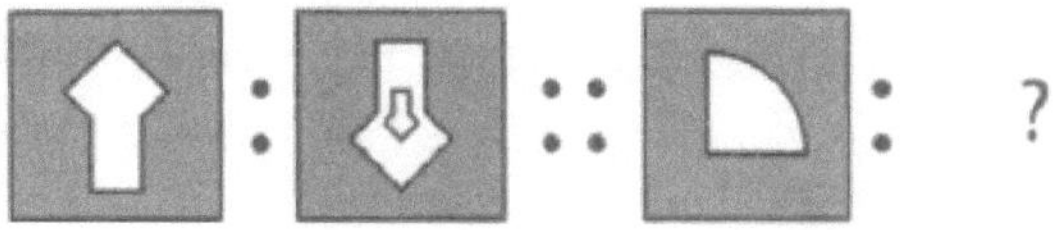

(A)  (B) 

(C)  (D) 

15. Choose the figure that will complete the series.

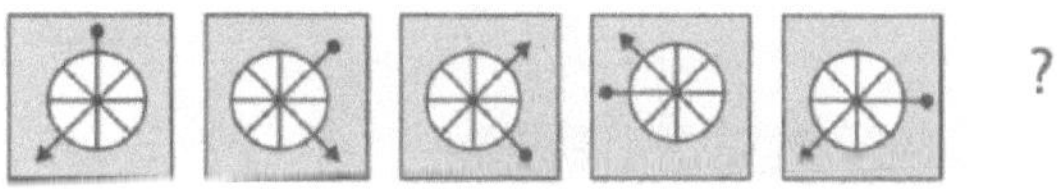

(A)  (B) 

(C) 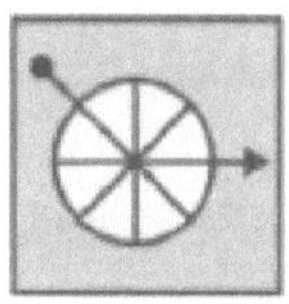 (D) 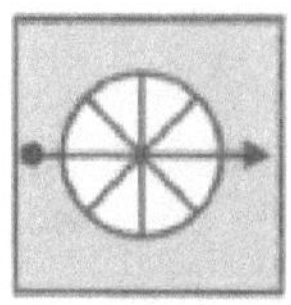

MATHEMATICAL REASONING

16. The following observations have been arranged in the ascending order. If the median of the data 29, 32, 48, 50, x, $x + 2$, 72, 78, 84, 95 is 63, then find the value of x.

(A) 46 (B) 54
(C) 62 (D) 80

17. Find the number of planks of dimensions (4 m × 50 cm × 20 cm) that can be stored in a pit which is 16 m long, 12m wide and 4 m deep.

(A) 1920 (B) 1220
(C) 1605 (D) 2040

18. The perimeter of an isosceles triangle is 32 cm. The ratio of one of the equal sides to its base is 3 : 2. Find the area of the triangle.

(A) $32\sqrt{2}$ cm^2 (B) 44 cm^2
(C) 48 cm^2 (D) 36 cm^2

19. In the given figure, O is the centre of the circle and ∠BDC = 42°. Find the measure of∠BAC.

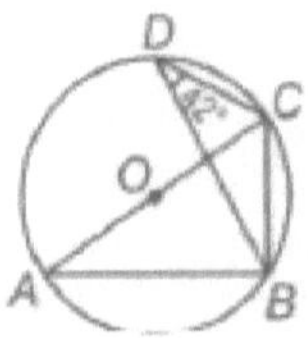

(A) 32° (B) 135°
(C) 42° (D) 85°

20. In the given figure, if AC = BD, then ______.

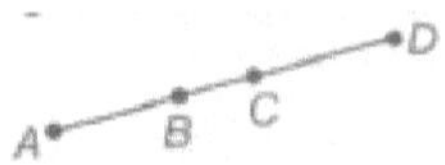

(A) AB = CD
(B) BC = CD
(C) AB = BD
(D) None of these

21. If the perpendicular distance of a point M from x- axis is 10 units, then the point M has ______.

(A) x - coordinate = –10 or 10
(B) y -coordinate = 10 or –10
(C) y - coordinate = –10
(D) None of these

22. Find the remainder when the expression $3x^2 + 8x^2 - 6x + 1$ is divided by $x + 3$.

(A) 11 (B) 4
(C) 6 (D) 10

23. The perimeter of a circle is equal to the perimeter of a square. Then, find the ratio of their areas.

(A) 14 : 11 (B) 10 : 2
(C) 7 : 1 (D) None of these

24. A person's present age is two-fifth of the age of his mother. After 8 years, he will be half of the age of his mother. How old is the mother at present ?

(A) 72 years (B) 40 years
(C) 58 years (D) 62 years

25. The edge of a cube is 40 cm. How many small cubes of edge 8 cm can be formed from this cube?

(A) 28 (B) 42
(C) 125 (D) 100

26. If $49x^2 - b = \left(7x + \frac{1}{2}\right)\left(7x - \frac{1}{2}\right)$, then find the value of b.

(A) 2/3 (B) $\frac{1}{\sqrt{2}}$
(C) 1/5 (D) 1/4

27. A cone is 8.4 cm high and the radius of its base is 2.1 cm. It is melted and recast into a sphere. Find the radius of the sphere.

(A) 4.6 cm (B) 9.4. cm
(C) 2.1 cm (D) None of these

28. In the given figure (not drawn to scale), ABCD is a trapezium in which AB = 7 cm, AD = BC = 5 cm, DC = x cm and the distance between AB and DC is 4 cm. Then find the value of x.

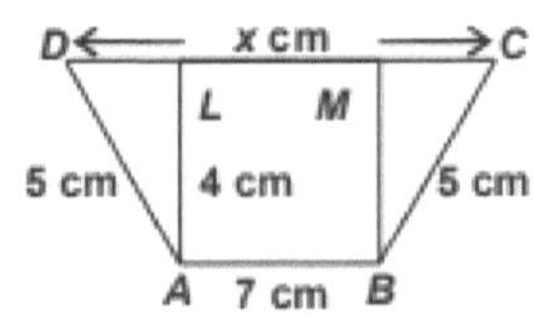

(A) 17 cm (B) 16 cm
(C) 13 cm (D) 15 cm

29. If $m = \frac{\sqrt{3}+\sqrt{2}}{\sqrt{3}-\sqrt{2}}$ and $n = \frac{\sqrt{3}-\sqrt{2}}{\sqrt{3}+\sqrt{2}}$, then find the value of $m^2 + n^2$.

(A) 98 (B) 48
(C) 62 (D) 0

30. In the rectangular coordinate system given-below, the shaded region is bounded by two straight lines. Which of the following is not an equation of one of the boundary lines?

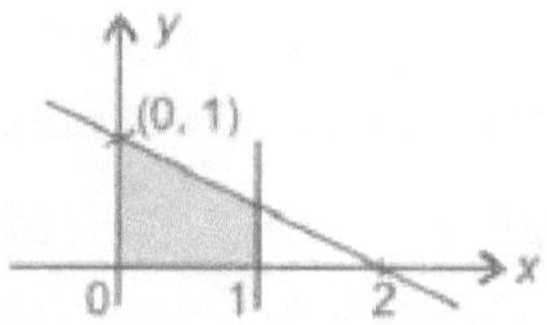

(A) $x = 0$ (B) $x - y = 0$
(C) $x = 1$ (D) $x + 2y = 2$

31. ABCD is a rhombus with ∠ABC= 56°, then find ∠ACD.

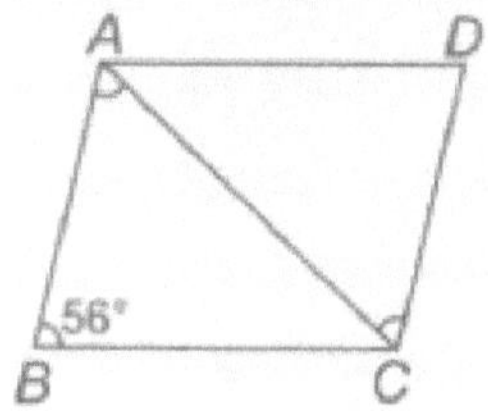

(A) 80° (B) 108°
(C) 62° (D) 26°

32. In the given figure, AB || CD. Find the value of x.

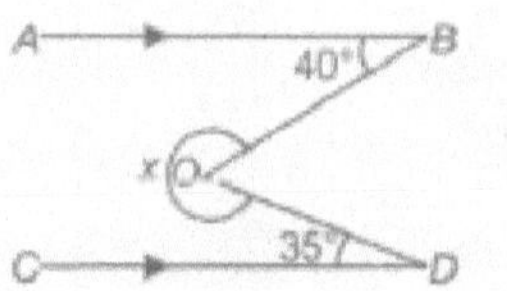

(A) 159° (B) 285°
(C) 300° (D) 260°

33. In the given figure, AD is the bisector of ∠A and AB = AC. Then ΔACD and ΔABD are congruent by which criterion?

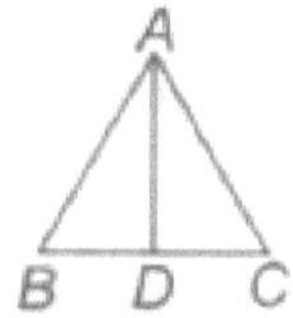

(A) AAA (B) RHS
(C) SAS (D) None of these

34. In the given figure, if ar (ΔABC) = 28 cm², then find ar (AEDF).

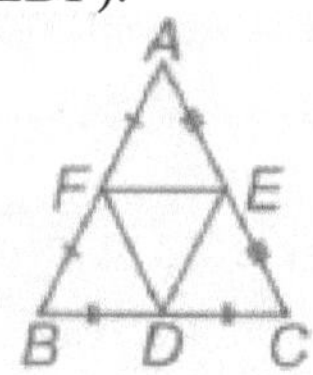

(A) 12 cm² (B) 8 cm²
(C) 14cm² (D) 34cm²

35. A card is drawn at random from a well shuffled pack of 52 cards. Find the probability that the card drawn is neither a red card nor a queen.

(A) 2/13 (B) 5/3
(C) 6/13 (D) 1/13

EVERYDAY MATHEMATICS

36. A hollow garden roller of height 63 cm, with a girth of 440 cm is made of iron 4 cm thick. Find the volume of the iron used.

(A) 107712 cm³
(B) 56892 cm³
(C) 256963 cm³
(D) None of these

37. A bag contains 8 red balls, 5 white balls, 12 green balls and 15 yellow balls. Reshu draws one ballfrom it randomly and found it to be white. Find the probability of drawing white ball from the bag.

(A) 3/10 (B) 1/8
(C) 7/30 (D) None of these

38. Tanya wants to level a ground which is triangular in shape having the sides 51 m, 37 m, 20 m. How much she has to pay if the cost of levelling is ₹ 3 per m².

(A) ₹ 918 (B) ₹ 920
(C) ₹ 1040 (D) None of these

39. A trader marks his goods 25% above the cost price. He then sells them at a discount of 25%. If the cost price is ₹ 500, then find the loss or gain percentage.

(A) 5.25% Loss (B) 7.15% Gain
(C) 6.25% Loss (D) None of these

40. Length, breadth and height of a cuboidal tank are $(x - 3y)$m, $(x + 3y)$m and $(x^2 + 9y^2)$ m respectively. Find the volume of the tank.

(A) $\left(x^3 + 3xy + 27y^3\right)\text{m}^3$

(B) $\left(x^4 - 81y^4\right)\text{m}^3$

(C) $\left(x^4 + 2x^2y^2 + 81y^4\right)\text{m}^3$

(D) $\left(x^4 + 81y^4\right)\text{m}^3$

41. Ashima has to paint a triangular cardboard for her project whose edges are 6 cm, 8 cm, 10 cm. Find the cost of painting it at the rate of 9 paisa per cm^2.

(A) ₹ 2.00 (B) ₹ 2.16
(C) ₹ 2.48 (D) ₹ 3.00

42. The compound interest on a certain sum for 2 years at 10% per annum is ₹ 525. Find the simple interest on the same sum for double the time at half the rate percent per annum.

(A) ₹ 500 (B) ₹ 1500
(C) ₹ 2600 (D) None of these

43. How many metres of cloth, 5 m wide, will be required to make a conical tent, the radius of whose base is 7 m and heightis 24 m?

(A) 150 m (B) 186 m
(C) 620 m (D) 110 m

44. Amal and Sahaj are friends. Each has some money. If Amal gives ₹ 30 to Sahaj, then Sahaj will have twice the money left with Amal. But, if Sahaj gives ₹ 10 to Amal, then Amal will have thrice as much as is left with Sahaj. How much money does Amal and Sahaj have ?

(A) ₹ 60, ₹ 30 (B) ₹ 62, ₹ 34
(C) ₹ 90, ₹ 70 (D) None of these

45. In a class test, in Social Science, 10 students scored 75 marks, 12 students scored 60 marks, 8 students scored 40 marks and 3 students scored 30 marks. Find their mean score.

(A) 42 marks (B) 68 marks
(C) 57 marks (D) 24 marks

ACHIEVERS SECTION

46. ABC is a right angled triangle with AB = AC. Bisector of ∠A meets BC at D. Then ________.

(A) BC = 1/2 AD (B) 2AB = BC
(C) BC = 2AD (D) None of these

47. If AB || CD and CD || EF. Also EA ⊥ AB. If ∠ BEF = 55°, find the values of x, y and z.

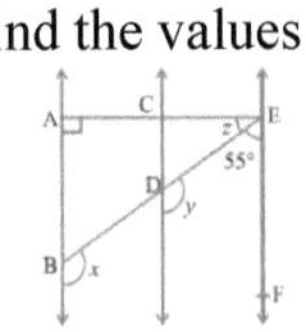

(A) 125°, 125°, 35°
(B) 135°, 140°, 165°
(C) 35°, 150°, 75°
(D) None of these

48. Sapna is playing with building blocks, which are of the shape of cubes, has built a structure as shown in the figure given below. If the edge of each cube is 5 cm, find the volume of the structure built by her.

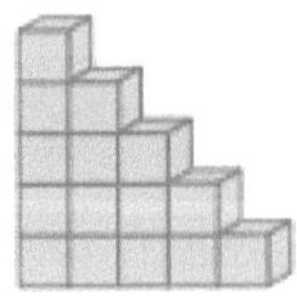

(A) 405 cm^3
(B) 1250 cm^3
(C) 1875 cm^3
(D) None of these

49. Match the following.

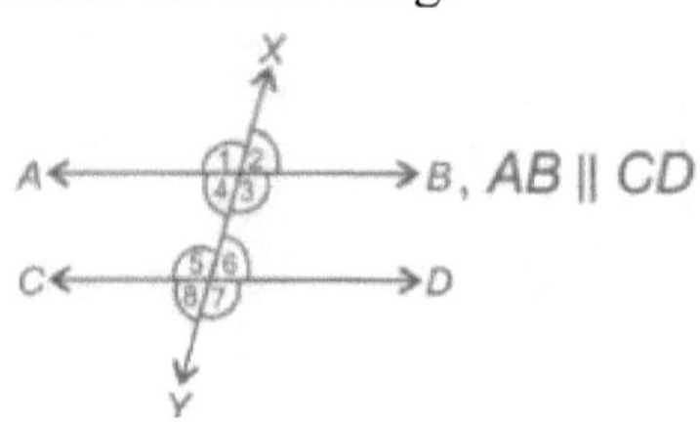

	Column I		Column II
a.	Alternate interior angles	(i)	$\angle 3 + \angle 6 = 180°$
b.	Co-interior angles	(ii)	$\angle 2 = \angle 6$
c.	Corresponding angles	(iii)	$\angle 2 = \angle 4$
d.	Vertically opposite angles	(iv)	$\angle 3 = \angle 5$

(A) a-(i), b-(iv), c-(iii), d-(ii)
(B) a-(ii), b-(iv), c-(i), d-(iii)
(C) a-(iv), b-(i), c-(ii), d-(iii)
(D) a-(iii), b-(ii), c-(i), d-(iv)

50. Anu has a piece of canvas whose area is 551 m^2. She uses it to have a conical tent made, with a base radius of 7 m. Assuming that all the stitching margins and the wastage incurred while cutting, amounts to approximately 1 m^2, find the volume of the tent that can be made with it.

(A) 1602 m^3
(B) 1232 m^3
(C) 880 m^3
(D) 2530 m^3

NATIONAL SCIENCE OLYMPIAD (NSO)

Mock Test Paper 1

NSO
NATIONAL SCIENCE OLYMPIAD

Total Questions : 50 Time : 1 Hour

PATTERN AND MARKING SCHEME			
Section	**(1) Logical Reasoning**	**(2) Science**	**(3) Achievers Section**
No. of Questions	10	35	5
Marks per Questions	1	1	3

SYLLABUS

Section – 1: Verbal and Non- verbal reasoning

Section – 2: Motion, Force and Laws of Motion, Gravitation, Work and Energy, Sound, Matter in Our Surroundings, Is Matter Around Us Pure, Atoms and Molecules, Structure of Atom, Cell-The Fundamental Unit of Life, Tissues, Diversity in Living Organisms, Why Do We Fall III, Natural Resources, Improvement in Food Resources.

Section – 3: Higher Order Thinking Questions – Syllabus as per Section – 2.

LOGICAL REASONING

1. Identify the mirror image of the given figure.

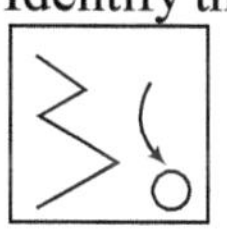

(A)  (B) 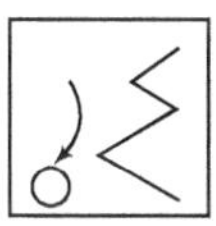

(C)  (D) 

2. Identify the figure which satisfies the same conditions of the placement of dots as in the given figure.

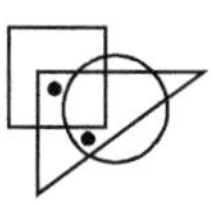

(A)  (B) 

(C) 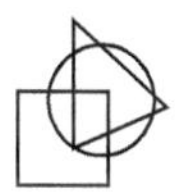 (D) 

3. By using one figure only once group the given figure into three classes.

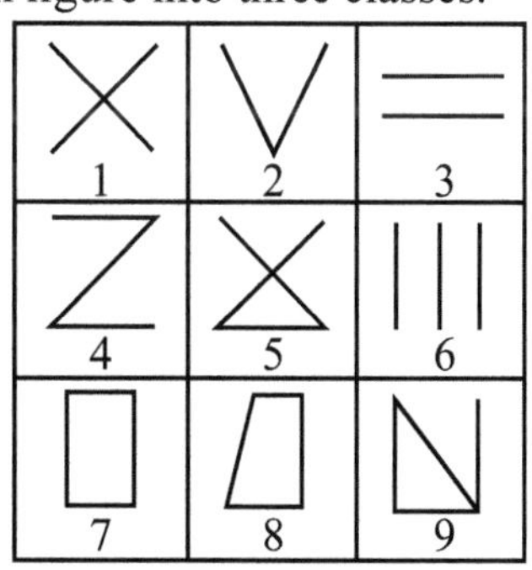

(A) 7, 8, 9 : 4, 5, 6 : 1, 2, 3
(B) 1, 4, 7 : 2, 5, 8 : 3, 6, 9
(C) 3, 5, 7: 1, 5, 9 : 4, 5, 9

4. Identify the image which will resemble to the unfolded form of the given image.
In the given image dotted lines represent the folding of the paper.

(A)  (B) 

(C)  (D) 

5. Select the figure which is suitable for the continuity of the series as given.

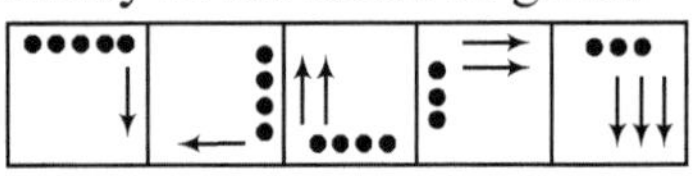

(A) 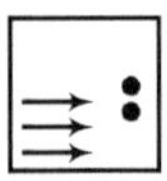 (B) 

(C) 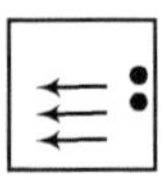 (D) 

6. Find the odd one out.

	X	Y
(A)	90	270
(B)	27	71
(C)	49	147
(D)	56	112

7. A group of 7 friends are sitting in a straight line. The group includes Garima, Fatima, Eklavya, Dane, Cate, Bhanu and Amisha. Now, carefully read the following arrangements.

A girl is sitting on the third to the left of Dane and at an end of the row.
Eklavya is immediate left to Fatima
Eklavya is sitting at 4th to the right of Garima.
Bhanu and Dane are the neighbours of Cate.

Determine the names sitting on the left of Cate.
(A) Eklavya and Dane
(B) Bhanu and Garima
(C) Fatima and Amisha
(D) Garima and Fatima

8. Nilesh, Dev, Ankur, Pintu and Kumar are friends and standing in a queue facing North. Carefully read the following information.

Dev is standing 60 m away in the South of Kumar.

Pintu is in the North of Dev and distance between them is 90 m.
Ankur is 40 m left of Kumar
Ankur is at 25 m East of Nilesh.

Determine the person in West and left to Kumar.
(A) Pintu (B) Nilesh
(C) Ankur (D) Dev

9. Let's assume today is your best friend's birthday. 2 years from today your best friend will be twice as old as your friend was 8 years ago. How old is your best friend today?
(A) 10 (B) 8
(C) 18 (D) 4

10. Which number can replace the question mark in the following figure?

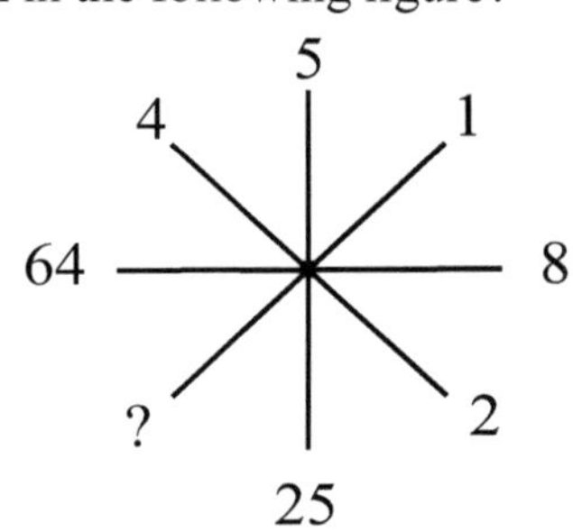

(A) 4 (B) 3
(C) 2 (D) 1

11. Mark the correct ascending order of densities of the given substances.
   (A) Air < Smoke < Wool < Iron < Honey
   (B) Wool < Iron < Honey < Air < Smoke
   (C) Honey < Air < Smoke < Wool < Iron
   (D) Honey < Air < Smoke < Wool <Iron

12. Identify the correct set of statements among the following statements.
   a: Under normal atmospheric conditions dry ice can easily be converted into gaseous state.
   b: For a substance its latent heat of fusion is generally lower than its latent heat of vaporization.
   c: As the state of a substance changes, its temperature also changes.
   d: Higher boiling point of the liquid indicates weaker intermolecular forces.
   (A) Only a and b
   (B) Only b and c
   (C) Only b and d
   (D) All are correct

13. Identify the incorrect statement(s).
   (A) To detect the drugs in the blood chromatography technique can be performed.
   (B) To separate cream and butter, centrifugation can be performed.
   (C) To separate camphor and salt, crystallization process is used.
   (D) To separate the coloured content of ink, evaporation process can be performed.

14. Following is a list of boiling points of certain gases, on the basis of the data identify the correct order of the gases distilling out from a liquid mixture.

Element	**Boiling point (°C)**
Nitrogen	196
Oxygen	183
Neon	246
Krypton	152

   (A) Nitrogen, Oxygen, Krypton, Neon
   (B) Oxygen, Krypton, Neon, Nitrogen
   (C) Krypton, Neon, Nitrogen, Oxygen
   (D) Neon, Nitrogen, Oxygen, Krypton

15. Among the following statements, identify the incorrect statement(s).
   a: Phosphorous is an example of polyatomic molecule.
   b: Phosphate ion is a positive ion and it shows trivalency.
   c: Aluminium ion is a positive and divalent ion.
   d: Calcium ion is positive and trivalent ion.
   (A) a, b and c (B) b, c and d
   (C) a, b and d (D) a, c and d

16. If a sample of ammonia has weight 8 g. What mass of SO_2 contains the same number of molecules as the number present in 8 g of ammonia.
   (A) 15 g (B) 30 g
   (C) 45 g (D) 60 g

17. Carefully observe the following table and mark the correct statement.

	Atom P	Atom Q
No. of Protons	6	6
No. of Neutrons	10	12

   (A) Atom P and Q are isobars of each other
   (B) Atoms P and Q show different chemical properties
   (C) Atom P and Q possess different physical properties
   (D) All of these

18. Identify isobars from the following table.

	P	Q	R	S
No. of Protons	20	18	20	18
No. of Neutrons	22	22	20	20

   (A) P and Q (B) Q and R
   (C) R and S (D) P and S

19. When a normal cell is placed in hypertonic solution (high concentration) ___ takes place and the cell _________.
   (A) Endosmosis, swells
   (B) Endosmosis, shrinks
   (C) Exosmosis, swells.
   (D) Exosmosis, shrinks

20. When a plant cell is placed in a hypotonic solution (less concentration), the cell does not burst. Why?
   (A) Cell wall prevents bursting.
   (B) Cell sap prevents exosmosis
   (C) The concentration of sugar inside the plant cell is higher.
   (D) None of these

21. Mark the incorrect statement.
   (A) Electron microscopes does not function at the principle of simple microscope, a high intensity beam is used in the place of natural light.
   (B) Active transport of the materials occurs against the concentration gradient and it involves ATP and various proteins.
   (C) Osmosis is a slowly occurring process, it occurs down the concentration gradient and it does not expand energy.
   (D) Solvents and solutes are not allowed to pass through a semipermeable membrane due to their size.

22. Identify the incorrect statement regarding the apical meristem.
   (A) Primary meristems are constituted of apical meristems.
   (B) Apical meristems bring about increase in length of the root and stem.
   (C) Dedifferentiation of the permanent tissues gives rise to apical meristems.
   (D) All are correct.

23. Identify the mismatched pair.
   (A) Stratified epithelium - Skin
   (B) Cuboidal epithelium – Kidney tubules
   (C) Cardiac muscles – Branched and multi-nucleated
   (D) Adipose tissues – Fat storage

24. Which of the following plant groups is known as 'amphibians of plant kingdom'.
   (A) Pteridophytes (B) Bryophytes
   (C) Algae (D) Fungi

25. Which of the following characteristics is not the criterion for the classification of animals?
   (A) Cell wall structure
   (B) Body cavity arrangement
   (C) Body symmetry
   (D) Presence of notochord

26. Mahira runs for 20 minutes at a uniform speed of 18 km/hr. At what speed should she run for next 15 minutes to maintain an average speed at 15 km/hr?
   (A) 11 km/hr (B) 12 km/hr
   (C) 1.1 km/hr (D) 1.2 km/hr

27. Read the passage carefully.

   We took two identical balls B1 and B2. Both balls are kept side by side at the bottom of a hill. After sometime B1 was kicked up the hill. B1 is headed downhill when it passes B2 headed up the hill.At the moment when B1 passes B2, it has the same:
   (A) Velocity and acceleration same as B2
   (B) Position and velocity same as B2
   (C) Displacement and velocity as B2
   (D) Position and acceleration as B2.

28. A truck and a car are moving with the same velocity on a horizontal road. Brakes were applied on the both moving bodies to bring them into rest, the brake provided equal retardation to both truck and car. Identify the correct result.
   (A) Truck and car will stop at the same distance.
   (B) Truck will stop at a shorter distance
   (C) Car will stop at a shorter distance.
   (D) Cannot be determines.

29. The rate of burning of fuel in a rocket is 2 kg/s, the velocity of the ejection of the fuel from the rocket is 30 km/s. Calculate the force exerted on the rocket.

(A) 300 N (B) 3000 N
(C) 30000 N (D) 300000 N

30. Match Column I and Column II

Column I	Column II
(a) Work done by the conservative forces	i. Change in kinetic energy
(b) Work done in uniform velocity	ii. Zero
(c) Work done by all the forces	iii. Change in potential energy
(d) Work done by external forces	iv. Change in mechanical energy.

	(a)	(b)	(c)	(d)
(A)	iii	ii	i	iv
(B)	iv	iii	ii	i
(C)	iii	ii	i	iv
(D)	ii	iii	iv	i

31. Let's say, an object at the height of h possess potential energy E_P= mgh. Identify the situation in which the equation is true.
    a. When the potential energy is dependent on the path
    b. When due to gravity the acceleration is constant.

(A) only a is true
(B) only b is true
(C) both are true
(D) none of them is true

32. Let's assume that the frequency of a source is 30 kHz. Identify the true statement regarding the frequencies of the sound waves produced by the source in air and water.

(A) Higher in the air
(B) Higher in the water
(C) Both in same medium
(D) Depends on the density of the medium.

33. The given graph represents the sound waves travelling in the medium. The sound source which is vibrating produces 480 oscillations in 120 seconds, determine the amplitude, frequency and the wavelength of the sound. (given velocity of sound = 348 m/s)

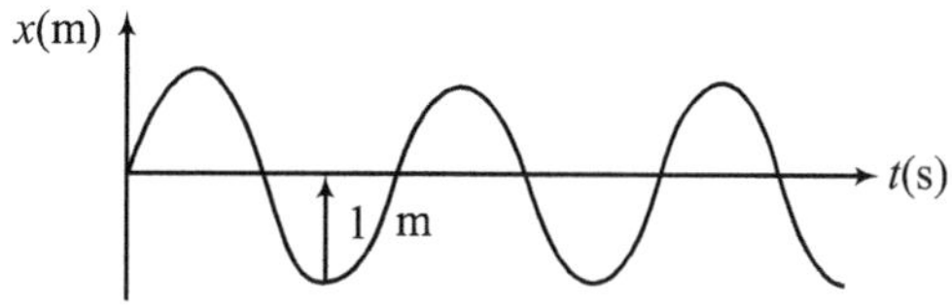

(A) 57 m (B) 67 m
(C) 77 m (D) 87 m

34. A recording studio is generally kept covered with the sound absorbent materials, why?

(A) To reduce the reverberation of the sound.
(B) To reduce the frequency of the sound
(C) To reduce the velocity of the sound
(D) All of these

35. An infected mother can pass on the pathogens of disease to foetus through ________.

(A) Placenta (B) Body Fluid
(C) Ovary (D) None of these

36. Carefully read the following statements and mark the correct option.
    P: Drastic long term effect are the main characteristics of the chronic diseases.
    Q: Antibiotics block the biochemical pathways of the bacteria, hence they resist and inhibit the growth of bacterial population.

R: Both male and female Anopheles are the vector of malarial pathogens.

(A) P and Q are true
(B) Q and R are true
(C) P and R are true
(D) All are correct

37. Why production of anti-viral drugs is difficult than the production of anti-bacterial drugs?

(A) Viruses are both living and non-living.
(B) Viruses possess an outer protein coat.
(C) Viruses exhibit fewer own biochemical process
(D) All of these

38. Match the column I and Column II

Column I	Column II
a. Fruits and vegetable peel	i. Physical water pollutant
b. Surfactants and detergents	ii. Air pollutant
c. Heat	iii. Degradable soil pollutants
d. Particulate matters	iv. Chemical water pollutants

	a	b	c	d
(A)	iii	iv	i	ii
(B)	i	ii	iv	iii
(C)	ii	i	iv	iii
(D)	iii	ii	iv	i

39. Identify P and Q.

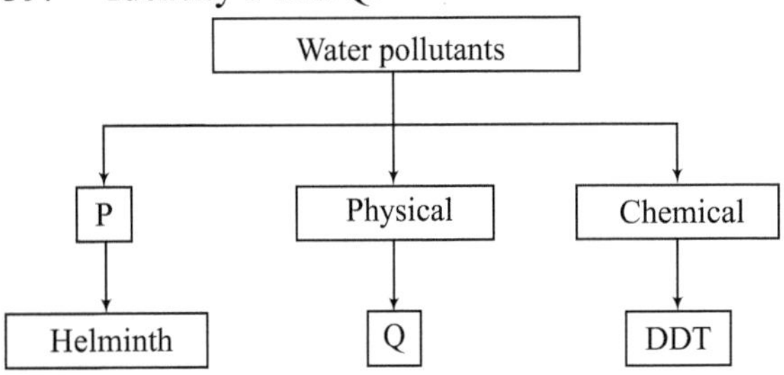

	P	Q
(A)	Ecological	Heat
(B)	Biological	Bacteria
(C)	Ecological	Fertilizer
(D)	Biological	Heat

40. Identify the incorrect statement about the rainfall with low pH.

(A) It affects the plants activities.
(B) Aquatic lives are largely affected by the low pH.
(C) Enhanced use of non-conventional source of energy results into the low pH of rain water.
(D) Sulphur and nitrogen oxide reaction results into the lower pH of rain water

41. In a food chain as the trophic level goes up, the concentration of non- biodegradable organic compounds increases. This phenomenon is known as ___________.

(A) Bioremediation
(B) Biomagnification
(C) Eutrophication
(D) Bioaccumulation

42. Identify the set of plant macronutrients.

(A) Calcium, magnesium, potassium
(B) Carbon, Hydrogen, Nitrogen
(C) Oxygen, Phosphorous, Nitrogen
(D) All of these

43. Blue revolution is linked to drastic increase in the production of ____.

(A) Aquatic life
(B) Milk
(C) Crops and cereals
(D) Ozone layer formation

44. Fill in the blanks with the suitable option.

__a__ is a draught breed of cattle.

__b__ is the production of hybrid by crossing two different species.

__c__ is manure which is produced in the field to provide some macronutrients to the soil.

	a	b	c
(A)	Gir	Interracial hybridization	Vermicompost
(B)	Sahiwal	Interspecific hybridization	Green manure
(C)	Nageri	Interspecific hybridization	Green manure
(D)	Gir	Interracial hybridization	Green manure

45. Several species of fish have different food habits, so they do not compete with each other for nutrition, therefore they can be grown in a single fish pond. Identify the mismatched pair of fish and its feeding habit.

(A) Common carp- Surface feeder
(B) Cirrhinus mrigala - Bottom feeder
(C) Labeo rohita - Column feeder
(D) Catla catla - Surface feeder

ACHIEVERS SECTION

46. Identify P, Q and R.

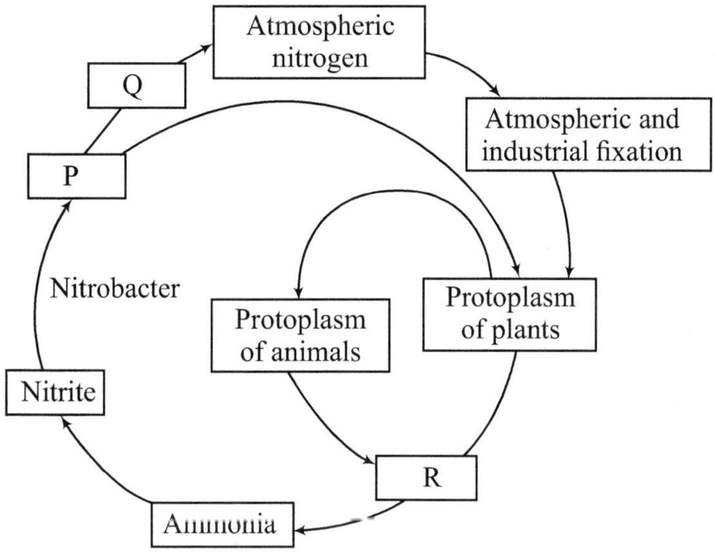

	P	Q	R
(A)	Nitrate	Denitrification	Ammonification
(B)	Nitrogen	Nitrogenation	Ammonification
(C)	Nitrate	Nitrogenation	Nitrification
(D)	Urea	Urea formation	Nitrification

47. Identify the set from the following which correctly explains the number of moles of each element present in 80 g of ferric sulphate.

[At. Mass of Fe = 56 unit, O = 16 unit and S = 32 unit]

	Fe	O	S
(A)	0.4	2.4	0.6
(B)	0.6	1.2	0.4
(C)	0.8	4.8	1.2
(D)	1.6	8.2	2.4

48. A hypothetical compound is made up of Carbon, Hydrogen and Nitrogen. These elements are present in the ratio of 12: 2.5: 14. If the molecular mass of the compound is 243, determine its molecular formula.

(A) $C_4H_{10}N_6$
(B) $C_{12}H_{30}N_{18}$
(C) $C_6H_{15}N_9$
(D) Cannot be determined.

49. Following are some keywords with respect to the key features of the cell organelles, relate them with the question and mark the correct choice.

a: Inner membrane with stalked particles.

b: Inner membrane which is connected to stacks like structures.

c: Small membrane less organelle which is composed of one small and one large subunit.

d: Hydrolytic enzymes are present in this sac like organelle

Identify the names of the organelles.

	a	b	c	d
(A)	Chloroplast	Mitochondria	Ribosome	Lysosome
(B)	Mitochondria	Chloroplast	Ribosome	Vacuole
(C)	Thylakoid	F1 particles	Nucleus	Vacuole
(D)	Stomata	Thylakoid	Ribosome	Lysosome

50. Observe the given flowchart carefully and identify P, Q, R and S on the basis of characters mentioned.

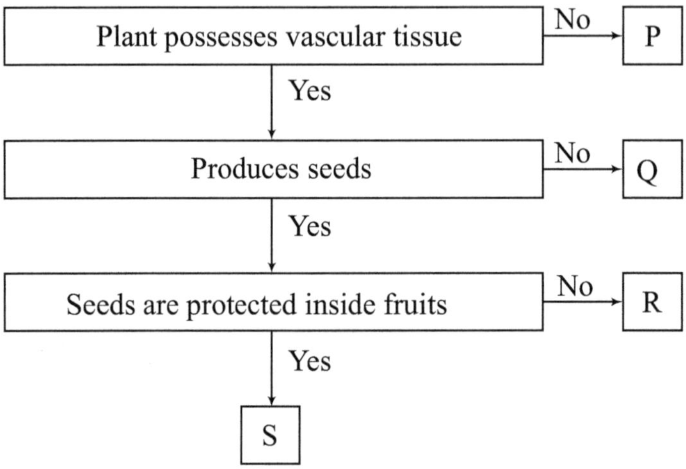

	P	Q	R	S
(A)	Redwood	Riccia	Ulothrix	Pines
(B)	Pines	Spirogyra	Dryopteris	Pines
(C)	Riccia	Marchancia	Ulotrix	Redwood
(D)	Liverworts	Equisetum	Pines	Ipomoea

Mock Test Paper 2

N S O

NATIONAL SCIENCE OLYMPIAD

Total Questions : 50 Time : 1 Hour

PATTERN AND MARKING SCHEME			
Section	**(1) Logical Reasoning**	**(2) Science**	**(3) Achievers Section**
No. of Questions	10	35	5
Marks per Questions	1	1	3

SYLLABUS

Section – 1: Verbal and Non- verbal reasoning

Section – 2: Motion, Force and Laws of Motion, Gravitation, Work and Energy, Sound, Matter in Our Surroundings, Is Matter Around Us Pure, Atoms and Molecules, Structure of Atom, Cell-The Fundamental Unit of Life, Tissues, Diversity in Living Organisms, Why Do We Fall III, Natural Resources, Improvement in Food Resources.

Section – 3: Higher Order Thinking Questions – Syllabus as per Section – 2.

LOGICAL REASONING

1. Identify, which of the following meaningful word can be made with the given word?

   CORRESPONDING

   (A) RESPONSE
   (B) CORRECT
   (C) DISCERN
   (D) REPENT

2. Read the following information carefully.

   Devika, Vandana, Niharika, Amisha and Kiran all collect key rings.

   Amisha has more key rings than Niharika

   Devika has twice as many as Vandana

   Amisha and Kiran have same number of key rings.

   Identify the correct option with respect to the given information.

   (A) Devika has fewer key rings than Amisha
   (B) Niharika has more key rings than Devika
   (C) Both (A) and (B) are true
   (D) Cannot be determined

3. In a certain language, P+Q mean 'P is brother of Q', P × Q means P is sister of Q and P : Q means P is father of Q. Identify the correct expression which indicates that X is uncle of Z.

   (A) X : Y × Z
   (B) Y × Z : X
   (C) X + S : R: Z
   (D) X + J : K × Z

4. Carefully observe the given Venn diagram and mark the correct option on the basis of following information.

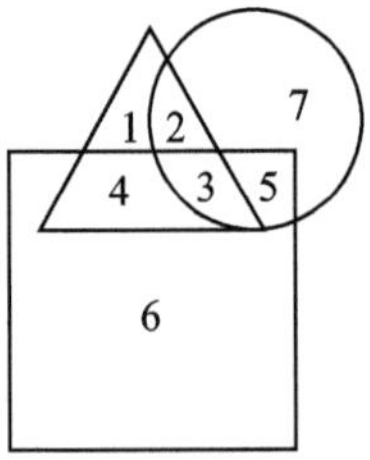

Triangle represents India, circle represents girls and square represents cricket fan. Determine which of the regions represents Indian non cricket fan girls.

(A) 2 (B) 3
(C) 4 (D) 5

5. Arrange the following words in a meaningful sequence.

P: Fruit Q: Flower
R: Branch S: Tree
T: Leaves

(A) T, S, R, P, Q (B) S, R, T, Q, P
(C) R, S, T, P, Q (D) T, P, Q, S, R

6. Identify the suitable set of figures which follow the given rule.

Rule: As the series proceeds its complexity increases.

(A) 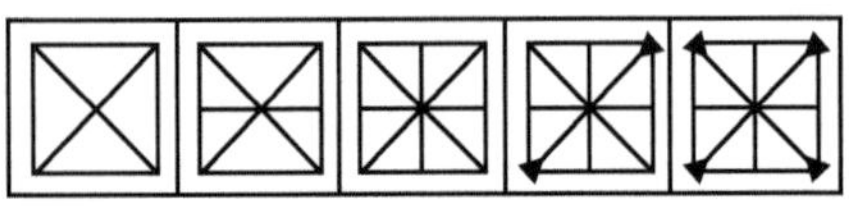

(B) 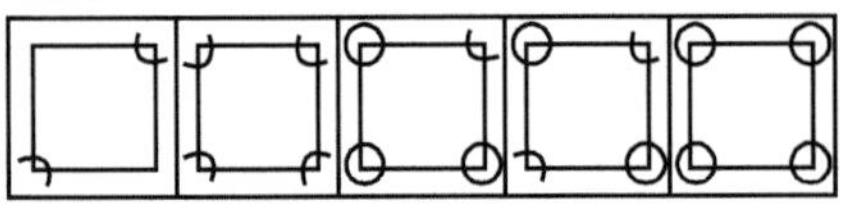

(C) 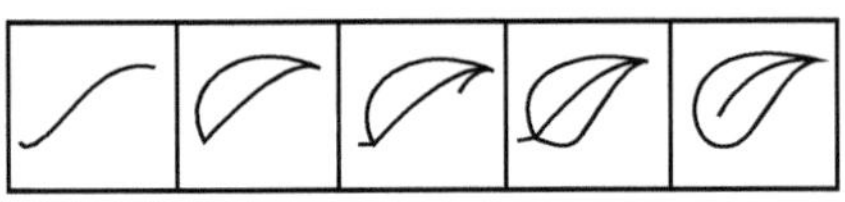

(D) 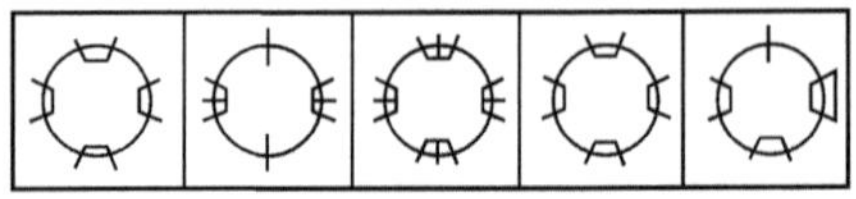

7. What would be the water image of the given figure?

(A)  (B) 

(C)  (D) 

8. Calculate the number of straight lines in the given figure.

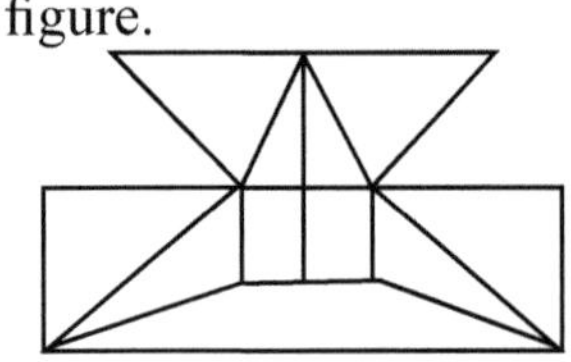

(A) 11 (B) 13
(C) 15 (D) 17

9. You often play with a dice. You threw the dice on the surface and the number showing on the top of the dice is 5, what would be the number on the opposite side?

(A) 6 (B) 4
(C) 1 (D) 2

10. Select three images from the following which will make a complete square if they are kept in the proper arrangement.

(A) 123 (B) 234
(C) 134 (D) 124

11. Find out the set of only micronutrients.
    (A) Nickel, Carbon, Chlorine
    (B) Nitrogen, Sulphur, Molybdenum
    (C) Copper, Zinc, Manganese
    (D) All of these

12. Identify the correct statement.
    (A) When two or more crops are grown in the same field simultaneously, this practice is known as intercropping.
    (B) In fewer cases fish culture is performed in the combination with rice crop.
    (C) Fish travels in the different zones of pond to gain food to make most efficient use of available food.
    (D) All of these

13. The given image belongs to the three different castes of honey bee colonies. Identity the incorrect statement.

    (A) Z is a fertile male known as drone.
    (B) X is a worker sterile female
    (C) Y is the queen bee which lays unfertilized (n) as well as fertilized eggs (2n).
    (D) X and Y emerges out from the unfertilized eggs while fertilized eggs develop into Z.

14. Identify P and Q.

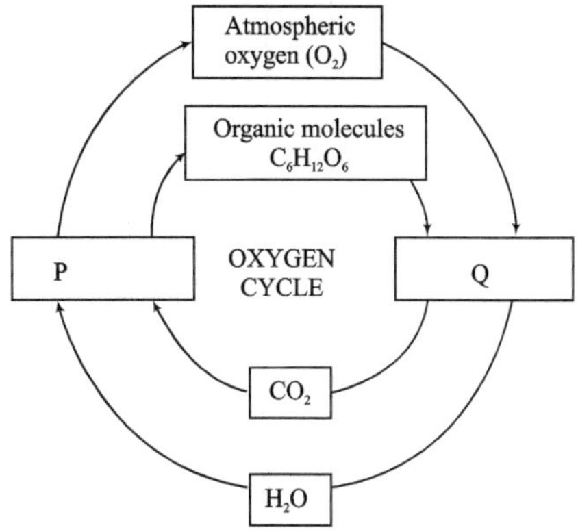

	P	Q
(A)	Respiration	Photosynthesis
(B)	Photosynthesis	Respiration
(C)	Respiration	Combustion
(D)	Photosynthesis	Combustion

15. Identify the activity which does not result into both water and air pollution.
    (A) Release of CFC from cooling bodies
    (B) Herbicides and pesticides being used in the crop fields
    (C) Factory wastes thrown into the water bodies
    (D) Burning of the fossil fuels

16. Eutrophication is the extensive growth of the algae into the water bodies which cause the reduction of dissolved oxygen amount into the water. Eutrophication is the result of which activity?
    (A) Bioaccumulation in algal species
    (B) Drastic change in the water temperature
    (C) Removal of factory wastes into the water
    (D) Extensive flow of nutrients into the water body

17. Mark the odd one out on the basis of mode of transmission.
    (A) Herpes (B) AIDS
    (C) Dengue (D) Syphilis

18. Mark the incorrect statement.

(A) DPT vaccine provides immunity against three different diseases.

(B) Edward Jenner developed a vaccine for the very first time in the history of vaccines.

(C) Vaccines provide permanent passive immunity against all kinds of pathogens as these are the antigenic protein preparations.

(D) A rod shaped bacterium causes tetanus.

19. Identify the structure and disease caused by this pathogen.

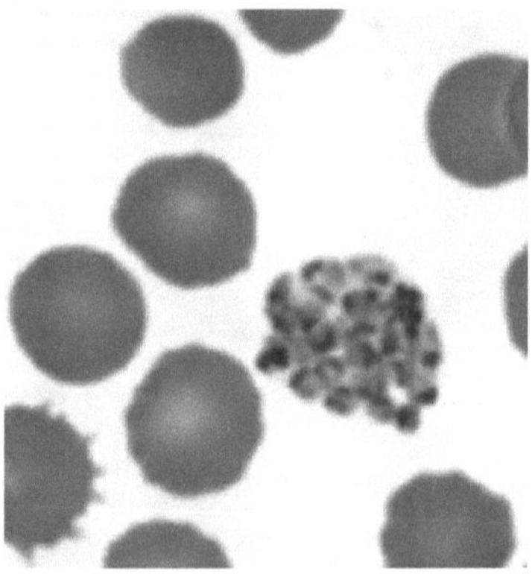

(A) Plasmodium vivax, malaria

(B) HIV virus, AIDS

(C) Chikungunya virus, chikungunya

(D) None of these

20. The medium which allows the travel of longitudinal waves is/are _____________.

(A) Gases (B) Solid

(C) Liquid (D) Any medium

21. Calculate the wavelength of the sound with the speed of 320 m/s and frequency 640 Hz.

(A) 2 m (B) 0.5 m

(C) 1 m (D) None of these

22. Carefully read the following statements and mark the correct choice.

S1: When sound waves collide with the hard surface, an echo is produced.

S2: Soft objects reflects the sound energy totally.

(A) Both S1 and S2 are true and S2 is correct explanation of S1.

(B) Both S1 and S2 are true but S2 is not the correct explanation of S1.

(C) S1 is true but S2 is false.

(D) Both S1 and S2 are false.

23. Carefully read the given statements and mark the correct option.

S1: The kinetic energy of an object varies as the square of its velocity.

S2: If two objects, one heavy and one light possess the same momentum, the kinetic energy of the lighter body will be higher.

(A) S1 and S2 are true and S2 correctly explains S1

(B) S1 and S2 are true but S2 does not explain S1

(C) S1 is true and S2 is false

(D) S1 is false and S2 is true.

24. A girl of mass 40 kg walks up to the temple which is situated 130 stairs up, each stair measures the height 20 cm. The girl reaches on the top in 100 seconds. Calculate the power of the girl. (g = 10 m/s)

(A) 80 W

(B) 100 W

(C) 104 W

(D) Cannot be calculated.

25. When a ball is dropped from the top of the tower which has height of h meters. The time taken by the ball to reach the ground was T. Determine the position of the ball in T/10 seconds.

(A) 99h/100 m

(B) 101h/100 m

(C) 100h/ 100 m

(D) Cannot be determined.

26. Mark the incorrect statement.
   (A) If an object is thrown up, at the top-most point the acceleration due to gravity is zero because the velocity of the object is zero.
   (B) Two small objects moving towards each other cannot be observed because the gravitational pull is balanced by the frictional force.
   (C) Both (A) and (B)
   (D) None of these

27. Mark the correct option.
   (A) An individual moving downwards in an elevator finds his weight less than his actual weight if the elevator is moving with constant speed.
   (B) Gravitation force exerted on an object is equal to the actual weight of the object.
   (C) Both (A) and (B)
   (D) None of these

28. Identify the correct option in the case of a ball rolling down on a slope with the steady speed.
   (A) The acting forces are balanced
   (B) The acting forces are unbalanced
   (C) The frictional force is higher than other forces.
   (D) None of these

29. A ball falls on the floor from the height of 30 m. The ball bounced upto the height of 15 m, if the ball touched the floor for 0.1 second, calculate its average acceleration.
   (A) 31.4 m/s^2 (B) 314 m/s^2
   (C) 41.4 m/s^2 (D) 414 m/s^2

30. Read the given statements carefully and identify true and false.
   P: If an object is moving in a straight path without reversing its direction, then their average speed is greater than the average velocity.
   Q: Distance can be referred as the magnitude of displacement in all aspects.
   R: If an object is moving with the constant velocity their average velocity equals to zero.
   S: If an object moves with the uniform speed, then the average speed is same as of instantaneous speed.

	P	**Q**	**R**	**S**
(A)	F	F	F	T
(B)	T	F	F	T
(C)	F	T	F	T
(D)	T	F	T	F

31. Identify the correct statement about dicotyledons.
   (A) Their flowers are mostly trimerous.
   (B) The vascular bundles in the stems are found arranged in a ring.
   (C) Their leaves show parallel venation.
   (D) Their root system is mostly consisting of fibrous roots only.

32. Read the given passage carefully and answer the question.
   Animal 'P' possesses four chambered heart and breathes through its lungs. These animals are cold blooded animals and possess scales. These are egg-laying animals and their eggs have tough covering and the eggs are well adapted to the dry terrestrial conditions. What is P?
   (A) Turtle (B) Crocodile
   (C) Frogs (D) Snakes

33. Carefully observe the image and mark the correct statement.

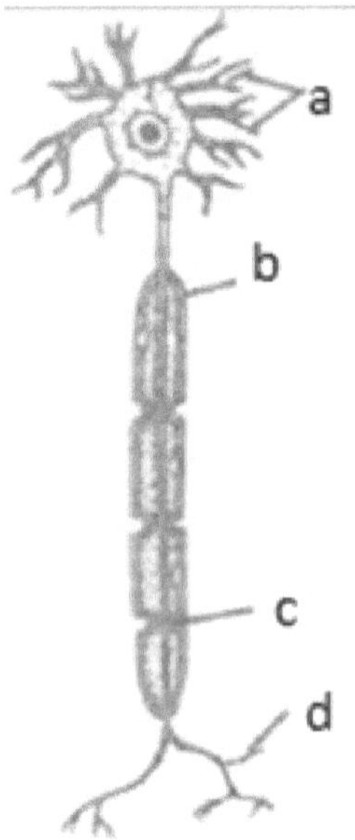

(A) a receives the impulse generated by b and eventually conveys it to the adjacent cells.

(B) d conducts impulse towards cyton while a conducts impulse away from cyton.

(C) c is named as node of Ranvier

(D) All of these

34. Correctly match column I and column II.

	Column I	Column II
P	Water conduction	(a) Sclerenchyma
Q	Mechanical strength	(b) Parenchyma
R	Food conduction	(c) Xylem
S	Food storage	(d) Phloem

	P	Q	R	S
(A)	d	c	b	a
(B)	d	b	a	c
(C)	c	d	b	a
(D)	c	a	d	b

35. Which of the following scientists discovered the cell?

(A) Robert Hooke

(B) Robert Brown

(C) William Hooke

(D) Darwin

36. Which of the following cell organelles is often termed as the traffic police of the cell?

(A) Nucleus

(B) Mitochondria

(C) Endoplasmic reticulum

(D) Golgi body

37. Identify the true and false statements among the following.

a: Acrocentric chromosomes are those chromosomes in which the centromere is situated near the end and its one arm is short in length.

b: During photosynthesis dark reaction occurs at granum and light reaction occurs at stroma.

c: Joint activity of endoplasmic reticulum and Golgi complex gives rise to lysosomes.

d: 70s ribosome can be subdivided into 50s and 30s subunits.

	a	b	c	d
(A)	F	T	T	F
(B)	T	F	T	T
(C)	T	T	F	F
(D)	F	F	F	T

38. Carefully read the given statements and mark the correct option.

S1: Bohr's orbits are also called as the stationary orbit.

S2: The moving electrons remain stationary in these orbits for sometime.

(A) S1 and S2 are true and S2 is the correct explanation of S1.

(B) S1 and S2 are true but S2 is not the correct explanation of S2.

(C) S1 is true but S2 is false

(D) S1 and S2 are false

39. Carefully observe the given elements and identify the correct statement(s).

Ar^{40}_{18}, Cl^{35}_{17}, K^{39}_{19}, Br^{80}_{35}, I^{127}_{53}

(A) The elements show difference in the order of proton number and reactive atomic mass.
(B) Ascending order of number of protons is Cl < K < Ar < Br < I
(C) Both (A) and (B)
(D) None of these

40. Choose the appropriate words to fill in the blanks of the following paragraph.

A formula which is used as the symbolic representation of the actual number of different atoms present in the molecule is known as _P_ formula. _Q_ is the representation of number of atoms of all the elements present in a molecule. The simplest ratio of the atoms present in one molecule of the compound is represented by _R_ formula.

	P	Q	R
(A)	Molecular	Valency	Empirical
(B)	Empirical	Atomicity	Molecular
(C)	Molecular	Atomicity	Empirical
(D)	Empirical	Valency	Molecular

41. As we know that the atomic mass of oxygen is 16 and molecular mass of ozone is 48. If ozone is an allotrope of oxygen, then calculate the atomicity of oxygen.
(A) 4 (B) 3
(C) 2 (D) 1

42. Suppose, you are performing an experiment. You mixed some iron filings and sulphur in a China dish and strongly heated them until you obtained a residue. Identify the property which does not belong to that residue.
(A) The appearance of the obtained residue is totally different from iron and sulphur.
(B) The obtained residue shows the chemical properties same as of iron and sulphur.
(C) The obtained residue cannot be separated into iron and sulphur by applying normal physical methods.
(D) The composition of the residue is not changed throughout the reaction.

43. Simran is a class 9 student. She was given a white compound to determine its melting point. In her experiments Simran found that the melting point is 110°C while her teacher told that the original melting point of the given compound is 120°C. Identify the reason behind the Simran's observation.
(A) The melting point of any white substance generally varies.
(B) The melting point changes with the amount taken for the experiment.
(C) Sufficient heat was not provided to the substance.
(D) The given substance must have mixed impurities, it is not pure.

44. Read the following statements carefully and identify the correct option.
S1: On exposure to the air, the state of solid CO_2 changes.
S2: Sublimation is shown by CO_2.
(A) S1 and S2 are true and S2 correctly explains S1.
(B) S1 and S2 are true but S2 is not the correct explanation.
(C) S1 is true but S2 is false
(D) S1 and S2 both are false.

45. Assume a substance S which has boiling point of 70°C and melting point of -30°C. Determine the physical states of the S at -100°C, 100°C and 0°C.
(A) Solid, Liquid, Gas
(B) Gas, Solid, Liquid
(C) Solid, Gas, Solid
(D) Solid, Gas, Liquid.

ACHIEVERS SECTION

46. Choose the correct option which shows the correct sequence of the steps for the production of new variety of the crop.
    (A) Germplasm collection → Selection of parents → Hybridization of selected parents → Selection of superior recombinants → Testing and release of new varieties
    (B) Selection of parents → Hybridization of selected parents → Selection of superior recombinants → Germplasm Collection → Testing and release of new varieties
    (C) Selection of superior recombinants → Germplasm Collection → Selection of parents → Hybridization of selected parents → Testing and release of new varieties
    (D) There is no fixed pattern

47. Niharika was standing facing a large wall. She starts clapping at a regular frequency of 20 Hz. She realizes that the echoes coincide with her clapping, mark the correct option regarding this situation. (speed of sound in air is 330 m/s)
    P: Time interval between two successive clapping is 0.05 s.
    Q: The distance between the wall and Niharika is 8.25 m in case she hears one more echo after stopping the claps.
    (A) Only P is correct
    (B) Only Q is correct
    (C) P and Q both are correct
    (D) P and Q both are incorrect

48. Carefully observe the given flow of process and mark the correct statement.

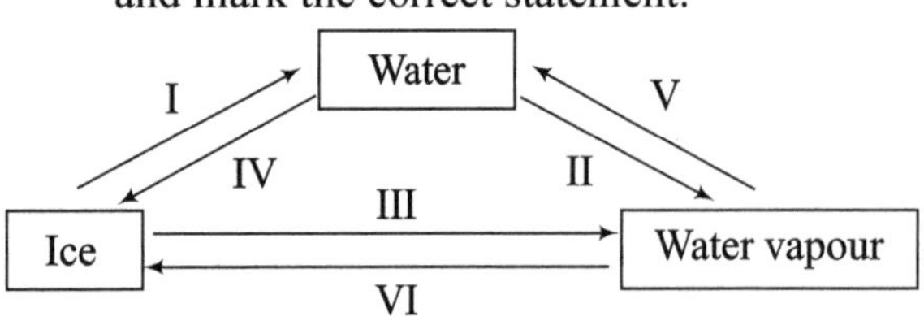

    (A) Endothermic process is represented by processes I, II, and III.
    (B) Exothermic processes are represented by IV, V and VI.
    (C) Latent heat for the process I is 3.34 × 105 J/kg
    (D) None of these

49. Observe the given Venn diagram carefully and mark the colloidal solution which ideally represent 1, 2 and 3.

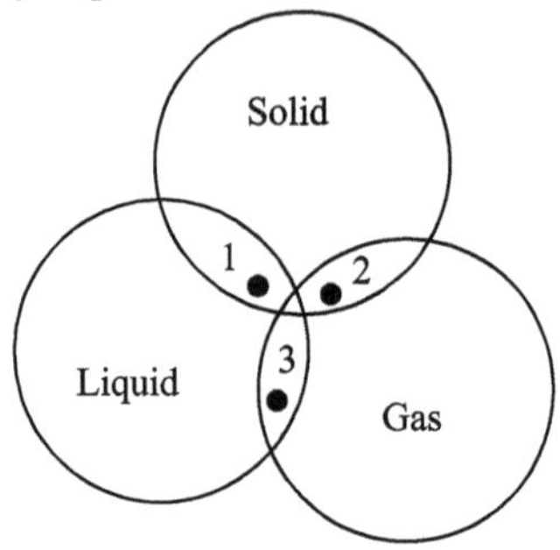

	1	2	3
(A)	Glass	Wings of honeybees	Oil
(B)	Paint	Smoke	Cloud
(C)	Mist	Cream	Fumes
(D)	Pain	Cream	Fumes

50. An object is taken, and it was made to float on water. When it was observed 1/3rd of its volume was above the surface of water. In another observation the same object was made to float in an impure alcohol. 2/5th of it was outside of the liquid. Calculate the relative density of alcohol.
    (A) 1.11 (B) 2.22
    (C) 3.33 (D) 4.44

NATIONAL CYBER OLYMPIAD (NCO)

Mock Test Paper 1

Total Questions : 50 Time : 1 Hour

N C O

NATIONAL CYBER OLYMPIAD

PATTERN AND MARKING SCHEME			
Section	**(1) Logical Reasoning**	**(2) Computer and IT**	**(3) Achievers Section**
No. of Questions	10	35	5
Marks per Questions	1	1	3

Section – 1: Verbal and Non-Verbal Reasoning.

Section – 2: Algorithms and Flowcharts in Programming, Visual Basic, Animations, HTML(Links, Anchors and Table tags), MS Word, MS Excel (Formula Auditing, Data Tools, Protecting and Sharing workbooks/worksheets, Working with cell range), MS PowerPoint, Hardware, Software, Input & Output Devices, Memory & Storage Devices, Flash CS6, Communication Technology (Networking, Internet and Multimedia),Operating Systems (Types-Interactive (GUI based), Real Time and Distributed, Commonly used OS), Using Windows 7, Latest Developments in the field of IT.

Section – 3: Higher Order Thinking Questions - Syllabus as per Section – 2.

LOGICAL REASONING

1. Choose the odd one out.
   (A) AAabc (B) AAabd
   (C) BBccc (D) AbdBC

2. IF YOU=19, and YUP=30, then 'MEN' is equal to
   (A) 14 (B) 4
   (C) 22 (D) 32

3. If A+B means A is sister of B; A−B means A is father of B, and A%B means B is A's wife. In the relation C%D+E−F, how does F relates to C?
   (A) Brother-in-law or daughter-in-law
   (B) Niece or Nephew
   (C) Son or daughter
   (D) Sister-in-law

4. A person arranges a given input of words following a particular rule in each step as follows:

   Input: consuming alcohol is injurious to health.

   Step I: consuming alcohol is injurious to.

   Step II: health Consuming alcohol is injurious.

   Step II: to health Consuming alcohol is.

   Step III: injurious to health consuming alcohol.

   What is the Step VI of the above word arrangement?
   (A) consuming alcohol is injurious to.
   (B) consuming alcohol is injurious to health.
   (C) to consuming alcohol is injurious.
   (D) alcohol is injurious to health.

5. In a certain region, three languages are spoken as follow:

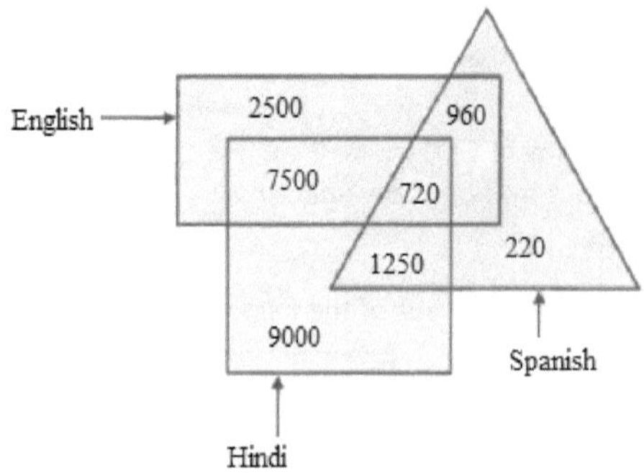

How many numbers of people speak both Hindi and English, but not Spanish?

(A) 19720 (B) 19000
(C) 7500 (D) 20250

6. A woman is facing towards North-East, and moves 10 m. She turns right and moves another 10 m. How far is she from his initial position?

(A) 16.44 (B) 12.36 m
(C) 14.14 m (D) 10 m

7. How many such digits are there in the following arrangement, each of which is followed by a letter, but not preceded by a numeral?

A 6 & 6 B 8 * C D E * 9 & 3 F 8 G $ H @ I 2 # 3 J

(A) 5 (B) 6
(C) 7 (D) 8

8. Choose a suitable figure from the option to replace the question mark (?) to form a series.

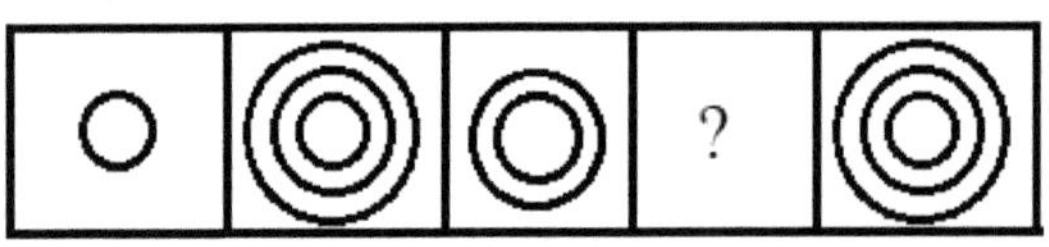

(A) 

(B) 

(C) 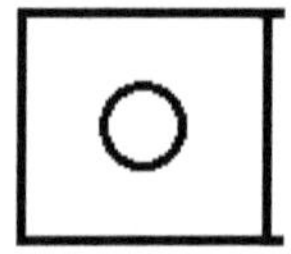

(D) 

9. Count the numbers of triangles in the given figure.

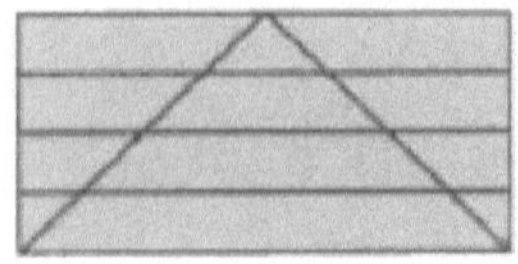

(A) 8 (B) 14
(C) 13 (D) 12

10. Find the water image of the following.

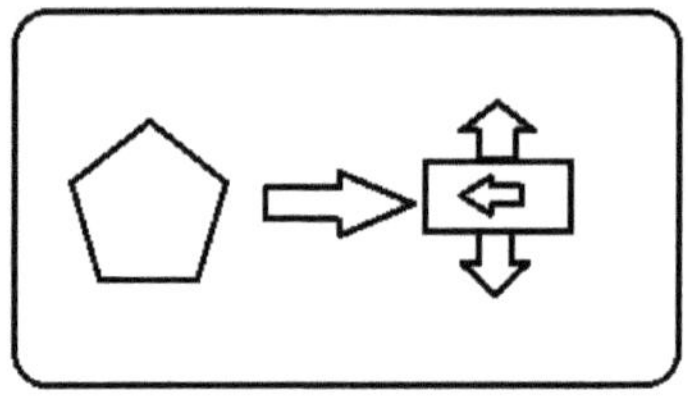

(A) 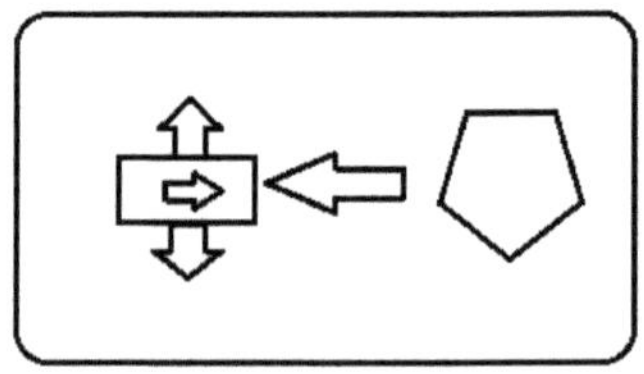

(B) 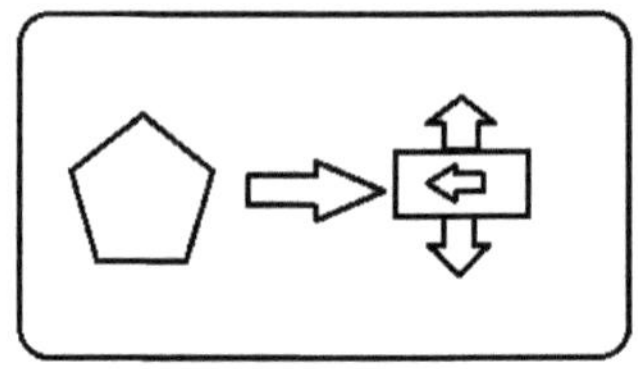

(C) 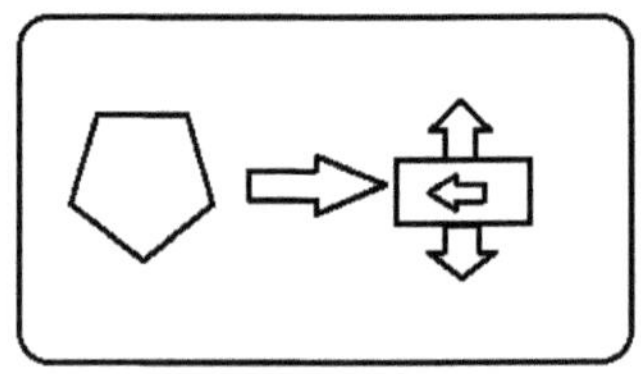

(D) 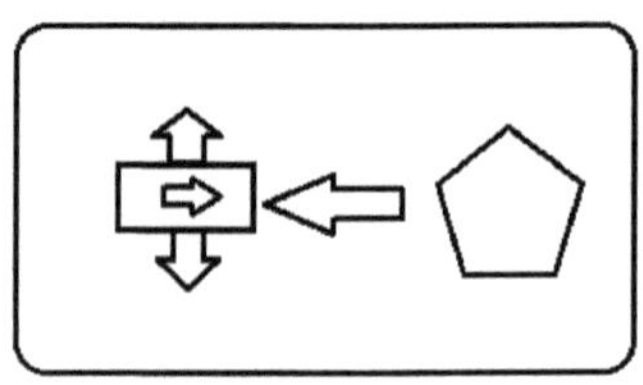

11. The code "<target>" defines _______.
(A) The link address.
(B) The link.
(C) Where to open the link document.
(D) The alternate link address.

12. The tag used to add rows to tables is _______.
(A) <ul> and </ul> (B) <tr> and </tr>
(C) <td> and </td> (D) <cr> and </cr>

13. Choose the odd one out.
(A) around (B) void
(C) hsides (D) box

14. The shortcut key "Ctrl + W" in MS Word is used to?
(A) Open document
(B) Switch between multiple word documents
(C) Close document
(D) Create new document

15. The feature of Microsoft Word that save information in every few minutes to ensure not losing of data is?
(A) AutoSave (B) AutoRecover
(C) AutoPreserve (D) AutoPrevent

16. In order to match the width of the MS word document with the width of the window, which of the following options is used?
(A) Match Width (B) Zoom Page
(C) Page Width (D) Spacing

17. What is the use of following shortcut key?

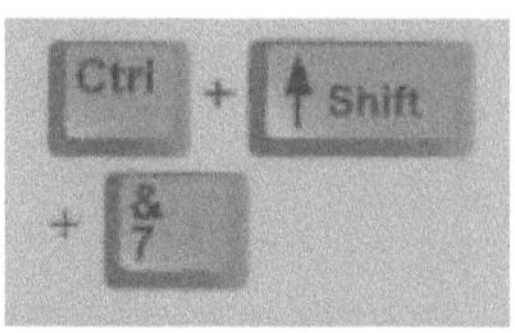

(A) Applies the outline border to selected cells.
(B) Unhide hidden rows within the selection.
(C) Applies the exponential number format with two decimal places.
(D) Removes the outline border from the selected cells.

18. The following icon is used for?

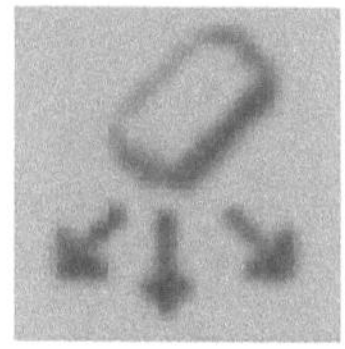

(A) It is used to remove arrows drawn by Trace Precedents.
(B) It is used to remove arrows drawn by Trace Dependents.
(C) It is used to trace errors.
(D) Both (A) and (B).

19. The _______ allows a user to debug a formula in MS Excel by executing each part of the formula individually.
(A) Examine formula
(B) Evaluate Formula
(C) Checking formula
(D) Auditing Formula

20. Which of the following icon is used for trigger in MS PowerPoint?

(A)  (B) 

(C)  (D) 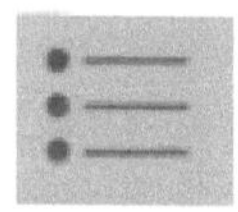

21. The shortcut key used for changing the font size in MS PowerPoint is?
(A) Ctrl + Shift + P
(B) Ctrl + Shift + F
(C) Ctrl + P
(D) Ctrl + F

22. The feature of MS PowerPoint that allows to combine copy of a presentation with its original presentation by accepting or discarding the changes into the presentation is?
(A) Research
(B) Track changes
(C) Custom animation
(D) Compare

23. Which of the following software can disrupt, damage, steal important data or gain authorized access to a computer system.
(A) Antiware (B) Malware
(C) Antivirus (D) Anti-exploits

24. The full form of VPN is?
(A) Virtual Private Networking
(B) Virtualized Public Network
(C) Virtual Private Network
(D) Virtual Public Networking

25. Which of the following technology is used to create a secure and private connection between two or more computer?
(A) SSL (B) FTP
(C) Bluetooth (D) VPN

26. The purpose of using DSL is _______.
(A) To transfer digital signals over standard telephone lines.
(B) To encrypts data before forwarding.
(C) To create wireless PAN.
(D) To create gateway for network.

27. The term used for time taken to pass a message from one node of network to other is?
(A) Broadband (B) Gateway
(C) Latency (D) Semantic

28. The device used to regenerate the network signal is termed as ______.
(A) Bandwidth (B) Router
(C) Modem (D) Repeater

29. Which of the following is a downloadable image recognition application developed by Google?
(A) Google Movies
(B) Google Goggles
(C) Google Images
(D) Google Picture

30. The term 'HMD' stands for?
(A) Heavy Metal Display
(B) Home Made Display
(C) Head Mounted Display
(D) Home Mode Display

31. A user observed that every time he turns on his computer, it shows incorrect time. He needs to replace _______.
(A) The BIOS
(B) The system board
(C) The CMOS battery
(D) The power supply

32. Which of the following is not a type of internal hard drive?
(A) SCSI (B) IDE
(C) EIDE (D) USB

33. The type of storage technology used to store the information on credit/debit cards is ______.
(A) Laser (B) Optical
(C) Magnetic (D) Holographic

34. Which of the following structure is used to allow operations to be repeated a fixed number of times?
(A) Sequential (B) While
(C) Loop (D) Selection

35. The instructions in algorithm are written from ________.
(A) Bottom to Top (B) Top to Bottom
(C) Left to Right (D) Right to Left

36. Which of the following flowchart indicates that the step is needed to be calculated manually?

(A) 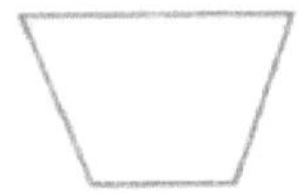

(B) 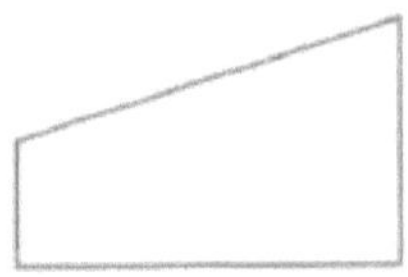

(C) 

(D) 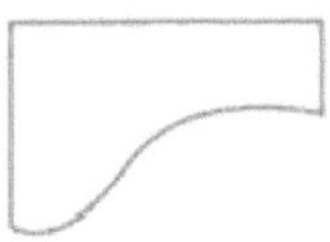

37. The method to stop an animated character for a specific number of frames is called as ______.
(A) Stopping (B) Slowing
(C) Freezing (D) Pacing

38. The full form of MIDI is?
(A) Musical Instrument Digital Identifier
(B) Multimedia Instrument Digital Identifier
(C) Musical Instructional Digital Identifier
(D) Music Instrument Digital Identification

39. Which of the following category of multi-media progresses without any navigational control?
(A) Non-Linear (B) Linear
(C) Non-contiguous (D) Contiguous

40. The symbol used for animating static images is ______.
(A) Scene (B) Static
(C) Instance (D) Graphic

41. The ______ tool is used to slow in or slow out the speed of an object in animation.
(A) Erasing (B) Curving
(C) Tweening (D) Flipping

42. Identify the following tool?

(A) Sub selection tool
(B) Lasso selection
(C) Free transform
(D) Shape tool

43. The full form of IDE in Visual Basic is?
(A) Integrating development environment
(B) Integrated development environment
(C) Integrated developing environment
(D) Integrating development entertainment

44. Which of the following is NOT a valid mode in Visual Basic application?
(A) Run mode (B) Interaction mode
(C) Break mode (D) Design mode

45. Choose the INCORRECT match.
(A) Int () – Converts a number into integer by truncating its decimal part.
(B) Frame – 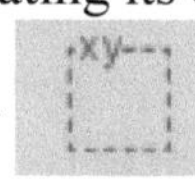

(C) Text box – 

(D) Label – 

ACHIEVERS SECTION

46. The following shown figure of a tool panel is categorised as _______.

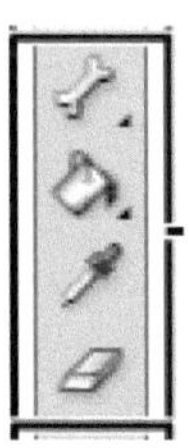

(A) Selection tools
(B) Drawing and painting tools
(C) Color and IK Bones
(D) Zooming and panning

47. What would be the output of the following HTML code?

```
<HTML>
<hr size=4 color=green width=50%>
<h1 align=center> THIS IS ME
</h1>
<hr size=4 color=green width=50%>
</HTML>
```

(A) 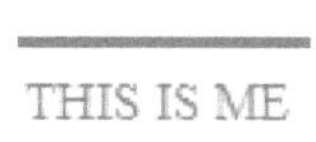

(B) 

(C) 

(D) 

48. Match the following.

	Column I		Column II
a.	Firewall	(i)	Protects information by converting it into unreadable code that cannot be deciphered easily by unauthorized people.
b.	Root Kit	(ii)	The technology that creates a secure and private connection between two or more computers.
c.	SSL	(iii)	A security system designed to protect a computer from hacker attacks.
d.	Disk Encryption	(iv)	Software used by attackers to gain administrative rights to a computer.

(A) a-(iii), b-(iv), c-(ii), d-(i)
(B) a-(iv), b-(i), c-(ii), d-(iii)
(C) a-(ii), b-(iv), c-(iii), d-(i)
(D) a-(ii), b-(i), c-(iii), d-(iv)

49. Which of the following statement is CORRECT about robust software?
(A) It is written in low level language.
(B) It can cope up data errors.
(C) It can used to control system performance.
(D) It is authorized to specific users.

50. Identify the error in the following flowchart used to calculate the area of a triangle.

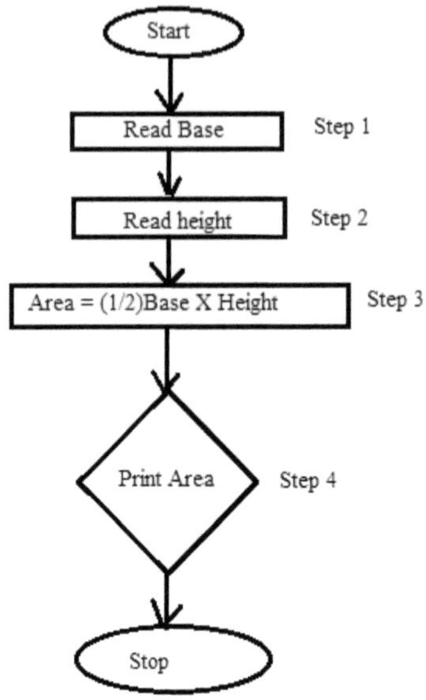

(A) Step 2 (B) Step 1
(C) Step 4 (D) Step 3

Mock Test Paper 2

NCO
NATIONAL CYBER OLYMPIAD

Total Questions : 50 Time : 1 Hour

PATTERN AND MARKING SCHEME			
Section	**(1) Logical Reasoning**	**(2) Computer and IT**	**(3) Achievers Section**
No. of Questions	10	35	5
Marks per Questions	1	1	3

Section – 1: Verbal and Non-Verbal Reasoning.
Section – 2: Algorithms and Flowcharts in Programming, Visual Basic, Animations, HTML(Links, Anchors and Table tags), MS Word, MS Excel (Formula Auditing, Data Tools, Protecting and Sharing workbooks/worksheets, Working with cell range), MS PowerPoint, Hardware, Software, Input & Output Devices, Memory & Storage Devices, Flash CS6, Communication Technology (Networking, Internet and Multimedia),Operating Systems (Types-Interactive (GUI based), Real Time and Distributed, Commonly used OS), Using Windows 7, Latest Developments in the field of IT.
Section – 3: Higher Order Thinking Questions - Syllabus as per Section – 2.

LOGICAL REASONING

1. Complete the following series.
   – 2, 0, _, – 2, – 6, _, – 8 ...
   (A) – 4, - 4 (B) – 2, - 6
   (C) – 4, - 2 (D) – 6, 4
2. In a certain code 'GOOGLE' is written as 'FQPHND'. How is 'CHROME' written in that code?
   (A) 'BISPND' (B) 'BJSPND'
   (C) 'BJSPOD' (D) 'BJSQOD'
3. Pointing to a man in a photograph, a woman says "He is the grandfather of son of my only daughter-in-law". How is the women related to the man?
   (A) Wife (B) Sister
   (C) Daughter (D) Grandmother
4. A, B and C are good in singing. B and D are good in dancing. A and C are good in athletic. B and C are good in badminton. Who among them are good in singing, dancing, and badminton?
   (A) B and C (B) A and B
   (C) B (D) C
5. A cyclist rides 300 m towards West. He turns left and rides 400 m. He again turns to North-West, and travels 500 m. He finally turns right and travels 600 m. How far the cyclist is from his initial position?
   (A) 625 m (B) 250 m
   (C) 300 m (D) 600 m
6. Arrange the following words in order in which they occur in a dictionary and choose the correct option sequence from the option.
   i. Assume ii. Assure iii. Assertion
   iv. Assumption
   (A) iii, i, iv, ii (B) iii, i, ii, iv
   (C) iii, ii, iv, i (D) iii, ii, i, iv

7. If 'A' denotes 'minus', 'B' denotes 'multiplication', 'C' denotes 'addition', and 'D' denotes 'divided by', then what is the value of the expression given below?

6B5C4A4B2D4

(A) 36 (B) 32

(C) 38 (D) 30

8. Select a figure from the four alternatives to replace the question mark (?).

(A) 

(B) 

(C) 

(D) 

9. What is the mirror image of the combination "M5A2N6G", when a mirror is placed into its left hand side?

(A) M5A2N6G

(B) 

(C) 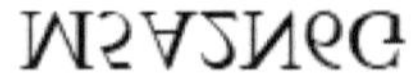

(D) 

10. A pattern and a dotted line are shown in the following transparent sheet. The sheet has to fold about the dotted line. Which of the alternatives figures best represents the pattern on the folded sheet?

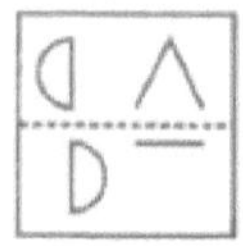

(A)  (B) 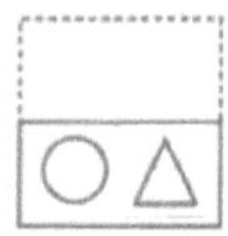

(C)  (D) 

COMPUTERS AND IT

11. The operating system that allows a user to click and drag objects with mouse instead of entering commands. The type of operating system is ______.

(A) CLI (B) GUI

(C) SSI (D) DSI

12. Which of the following statement regarding 'SDIO' card is incorrect?

(A) It enables devices to use SD slot to support Bluetooth adapters.

(B) It enables devices to use SD slot to support GPS receivers.

(C) It can be used for interface of input or output devices.

(D) It is a type of volatile memory card.

13. The flash CS6 is a type of _____.

(A) BIOS

(B) Multimedia software

(C) Power source

(D) Operating system

14. Consider the following statement:

COUNT = 25

ADD = ADD + COUNT

COUNT = COUNT −1

The above statement is examples of ______.

(A) Declaration statements

(B) Input statements

(C) Output Statements

(D) Assignment statements

15. The following flowchart is an example of __________.

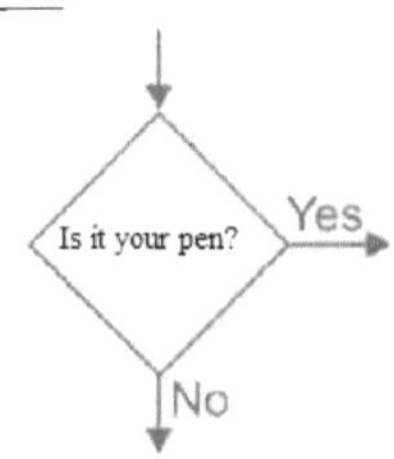

(A) Decision symbol
(B) Terminal symbol
(C) On page connector
(D) Off page connector

16. Which of the following statement is correct about an algorithm?
(A) It is a set of instruction to be followed before choosing a programming language.
(B) It is a help guide that instructs how to use software.
(C) It is a self contained step-by-step set of operations to be performed in the given sequence.
(D) It is a collection of symbol used to design a flowchart.

17. Which of the following procedure of graphics and image handling is used to turn one image gradually into another?
(A) Universal (B) Animation
(C) Morphing (D) Multimedia

18. The loudness of specific audio frequencies can be adjusted by using the _______ software or hardware.
(A) Acousters
(B) Compound meters
(C) Boosters
(D) Equalizers

19. It is an example of ______ media that allows users to go forward or backward while playing a movie through DVD.
(A) Linear
(B) Contiguous
(C) Non-contiguous
(D) Non-Linear

20. The flash has default frame rate of ______.
(A) 30 (B) 16
(C) 24 (D) 64

21. The tool used to scale, rotate and change the direction of the gradient fill in an object is _______.
(A) Polyster
(B) Gradient Transform
(C) Free Transform
(D) Gradient Fill

22. Choose the odd one out.
(A) Gradient glow (B) Gradient shadow
(C) Bevel (D) Gradient Bevel

23. The values of variable 'var' after execution is _______.
var = 3 − 2 Mod 1 +1 − 2
(A) 2 (B) 3
(C) 0 (D) 1

24. Which of the following function key is used to insert or toggles a breakpoint in visual basic?
(A) F1 (B) F3
(C) F6 (D) F9

25. Identify the following tool?

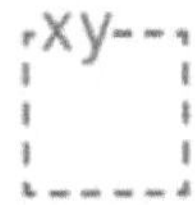

(A) Text box (B) Label
(C) Frame (D) Image tool

26. The attribute used to control the space between a cell's border and its contents is known as _____.
(A) Colspan (B) Cellpadding
(C) Rowspan (D) Cellspacing

27. A user writes a code as "<Body text = Black >". The motive of user is to?
(A) Change the text colour to black.
(B) Change the link colour to black.
(C) Change the background colour to black.
(D) Change colour of title text to black.

28. The tag used to add cells in a row of a table is ______.
(A) <col> (B) <cell>
(C) <val> (D) <td>

29. The key "Ctrl + Alt + C" in Microsoft Word 2010 is used to _______.
(A) Insert registered trademark
(B) Insert Copyright symbol
(C) Copy selected text or object
(D) Copy the header or footer from previous selection of the document.

30. To view all the changes in header and footer area of word document while tracking changes, we use _______.
   (A) Reviewing Pane
   (B) Research Pane
   (C) Changes Pane
   (D) Show Markup

31. The Pane used to search through a word document is?
   (A) Find Pane
   (B) Document Pane
   (C) Navigation Pane
   (D) Searching Pane

32. The use of the following icon is?

   (A) Edit the layout of the document
   (B) Save a set of display and print settings
   (C) To zoom in or zoom out the document
   (D) View the document in full screen mode

33. The shortcut key for AutoSum function of MS Excel 2010 is?
   (A) Ctrl + = (B) Alt + =
   (C) Ctrl + Alt + S (D) Ctrl + Alt + =

34. Using of COUNTA function will ________.
   (A) Return the number of non-blank cells in a range.
   (B) Return the correlation between two data.
   (C) Return the number of blank cells in a range.
   (D) Return the number of blank cells on the entire worksheet.

35. Identify the following icon of MS Power-Point.

   (A) SmartArt (B) Object
   (C) Edit comment (D) Trigger

36. Choose the correct match.
   (A) From Current Slide – 
   (B) From beginning – 
   (C) Custom Slide show – 
   (D) Hyper link – 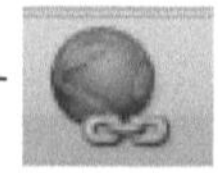

37. The shortcut key to switch between Slides and Outline pane in Normal View is?
   (A) Ctrl + Tab
   (B) Shift + Tab
   (C) Ctrl + Shift + Tab
   (D) Shift + F5

38. The full form of WLAN is?
   (A) Wireless Local Area Network.
   (B) Wireless Local Access Network.
   (C) Windows Local Access Network.
   (D) Windows Local Area Networking.

39. Which of the following device connects your computer to your phone line and provide access to the network?
   (A) BIOS (B) Repeater
   (C) Browser (D) Modem

40. The software that detects and removes viruses and other malicious software from the computer is?
   (A) Firewall (B) Antivirus
   (C) Nimda (D) Sapphire

41. The ______ is used to connect a computer to a hub or switch.
   (A) Axial Cable (B) Jack Cable
   (C) LAN Cable (D) Patch Cable

42. The animated movie "Finding Dory" is produced by __________.
   (A) Sony Picture Animation
   (B) Walt Disney picture
   (C) Pixar Animation Studios
   (D) Warner Bros. Animation

43. Which of the following options does not allow a user to create wireless PAN?
(A) Infrared (B) Bluetooth
(C) FireWire (D) Both (A) and (B)

44. The reason why the switches are preferred over hubs for networking is ______.
(A) Bandwidth is shared in switches.
(B) They give better network performance than hubs.
(C) Switch is cheaper.
(D) All of the above.

45. Nupedia is the predecessor of ________.
(A) Wikipedia (B) Google Chrome
(C) Opera (D) Twitter

ACHIEVERS SECTION

46. Consider the Visual Basic code "print ("Good-Morning"). If a user wish to obtain the output of the code as "Good/Morning", then which of the following function code must be used?
(A) Replace (B) ByVal
(C) ByRef (D) Alter

47. Choose the INCORRECT match.

(A)  – Insert common mathematical equations or create equations using a library of math symbols.

(B) 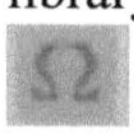 – Insert symbols that are not on your keyboard, such as copyright symbol, trademark symbol.

(C)  – Select text or object in the documents.

(D)  – Make text look like as it is marked with a highlighter pen.

48. A salesperson sells products in 10 different regions. The yearly sales from each region are stored in 10 identical worksheets. If the sales person wishes to calculate the total sales in a year from the entire region, then which MS Excel tool he must be used?
(A) Watch Window
(B) What-If Analysis
(C) Subtotal
(D) Consolidate

49. Which of the following regarding hub is INCORRECT?
(A) It connects several computers on a network.
(B) It does not conserve network bandwidth while delivering the message.
(C) It receives and transmits the data in a network.
(D) It is capable of checking data packets as they are received.

50. Match the following.

Column I		Column II	
a.	Pharming	(i)	It is a technique used for automatic extraction of useful information by image capturing and analysis.
b.	3D Printing	(ii)	It is a network discovery technology that allows user to setup a network without any manual configuration.
c.	Bonjour	(iii)	Rerouting from a requested site to an undesired site without intervention of a user.
d.	Machine Vision	(iv)	Additive manufacturing

(A) a-(iii), b-(iv), c-(ii), d-(i)
(B) a-(iv), b-(i), c-(ii), d-(iii)
(C) a-(ii), b-(iv), c-(iii), d-(i)
(D) a-(ii), b-(i), c-(iii), d-(iv)

INTERNATIONAL ENGLISH OLYMPIAD (IEO)

Mock Test Paper 1

I E O

INTERNATIONAL ENGLISH OLYMPIAD

Total Questions : 50 Time : 1 Hour

PATTERN AND MARKING SCHEME				
Section	**(1) Word and Structure Knowledge**	**(2) Reading**	**(3) Spoken and Written Expression**	**(4)Achievers**
No. of Questions		45		5
Marks per Questions		1		3

SYLLABUS

Section – 1 : Synonyms, Antonyms, Analogies and Spellings, One Word, Word Order, Nouns, Pronouns, Verbs, Adverbs, Adjectives, Articles, Prepositions, Conjunctions, Punctuations, Jumbled Words, Voices, Concord, Question Forms, Tenses, Conditionals, Modals, Reported Speech. Collocations, Phrasal Verbs, Idioms, Homonyms and Homophones, Words related to Social Cause, Travel, Workplace, etc.

Section – 2 : Search for and retrieve information from various text types like Flyers, Classifieds, Dictionaries, etc., Understand information presented in Instruction Manual Format, Message Format and others. Acquire broad understanding of and look for specific information in longer texts like Editorials, Essays, etc.

Section – 3 : Ability to understand situation-based variations in functions like Giving Advice, Stating Preferences, Discussing Probability, Making an Offer, etc.

Section – 4 : Higher Order Thinking Questions - Syllabus as per Sections 1, 2 and 3.

WORD AND STRUCTURE KNOWLEDGE

1. Choose the correct option for the given description.

   "Treatment or consideration of or making a distinction towards a person based on their race, age, sex or religion."

   (A) Incentive
   (B) Harassment
   (C) Discrimination
   (D) None of these

2. Which of the following words related to workplace?

   (A) Efficiency
   (B) Monitoring
   (C) Human Resource
   (D) All of these

3. Choose the correct description for the word 'Roadie'.

   (A) Someone whose job is to travel with musicians and move their equipment.
   (B) A list of passengers on a ship or plane.
   (C) A person who travels by walking.
   (D) Someone who travels around without a definite direction or purpose.

4. Comvplete the following sentence with suitable idiom.

   "By taking my wife on holiday, I killed____________. I got a chance to refresh myself but also spend time with her."

   (A) a piece of cake
   (B) two birds with one stone
   (C) see eye to eye
   (D) None of these

5. In the given sentence replace the blank with the correct option.

Raghav ____ working with us for three years now.

(A) have been (B) is
(C) has been (D) had been

6. Fill in the blank with suitable preposition.

Misha told her friend that her parents have been married _____ thirty years.

(A) for (B) since
(C) until (D) None of these

7. Choose the correct option.

Would you like me to ______________ you some lemonade?

(A) poor
(B) pour
(C) Both (A) and (B)
(D) None of these

8. Fill in the blank with suitable option.

Nisha's parents _______ her to watch a movie with her friend.

(A) aloud
(B) allowed
(C) Both (A) and (B)
(D) None of these

9. Fill in the blank with suitable article.

Gold is ______ precious metal. It is used to make ornaments and also used in dentistry for filling cavities.

(A) the (B) a
(C) an (D) None of these

10. Fill in the blank with suitable conjunction.

The sun was warm, _____ the wind was a bit too cool.

(A) but (B) and
(C) yet (D) None of these

11. Arrange the jumbled words to form a meaningful sentence.

from God / a precious / life / is / to / gift / us

(A) A precious gift to us is life from God.
(B) From God a precious gift to us is life.
(C) Life is a precious gift to us from God.
(D) None of these

12. Insert the correct word in the sentence given below.

There ___ lack of employment opportunities in rural areas.

(A) is (B) are
(C) was (D) None of these

13. Fill in the blank.

Unemployment is a ________ for the government these days.

(A) obstacle (B) major problem
(C) issue (D) None of these

14. Fill in the blank with suitable modal.

________ you please lend me your bag?

(A) Could (B) Would
(C) Ought (D) Can

15. Choose the correct punctuation.

Who do you think will win the trophy___?

(A) . (B) ?
(C) ! (D) ,

16. Choose the correct option to fill in the blank.

The music at the party was melodious, _______?

(A) were it (B) weren't it
(C) was it (D) wasn't it

17. Choose the most suitable passive voice conversions of the given sentence.

We are going to watch a magic show tonight.

(A) A magic show has to be watched by them tonight.
(B) A magic show is going to be watched by us tonight.
(C) We will go to watch a magic show tonight.
(D) None of these

18. Fill in the blank using correct phrasal verb.

Shweta ordered her maid to look ______ the children, so that she can go to the party.

(A) for (B) into
(C) at (D) after

19. Choose the most appropriate indirect narration of the given sentence.

The teacher said, "Be quiet and listen to my words."

(A) The teacher ordered them to be quiet and listen to his words.
(B) The teacher told the students to be quiet and listen to my words.
(C) The teacher said to them to be quiet and listen to my words.
(D) None of these

20. Replace the underlined words with appropriate adjective.

Esha used to show <u>very unpleasant, disgraceful and nasty</u> behaviour towards her colleagues, so they distanced themselves from her.

(A) optimist (B) obnoxious
(C) permissible (D) hazardous

21. Insert the suitable adverb of manner.

In the history of India, many female freedom fighters fought ____ against the Britishers.

(A) brutally (B) bravely
(C) virtually (D) quickly

22. Place the words in order to make a complete and sensible sentence.

A everyday library visit to I go

(A) I visit a to go library everyday
(B) Every day a I visit to go library
(C) I go to visit a library everyday.
(D) None of these

23. Complete the following sentence with the insertion of suitable pronoun.

I went for a picnic with my friends, but it was raining there heavily, therefore __ couldn't enjoy __.

(A) I, myself (B) They, themselves
(C) We, ourselves (D) none of these

24. Fill in the blank with suitable possessive noun.

Listen to your ______ advice seriously, otherwise you'll lose the match.

(A) mother's (B) father's
(C) coach's (D) friend's

25. Complete the sentence with the suitable proverb.

My car was _____ in the middle of the road.

(A) broken down (B) went off
(C) turned up (D) blown away

26. Fill in the blank with suitable words to complete the proverb which supports 'Swachh Bharat Campaign.'

Cleanliness is next to ______

(A) betterness (B) goodness
(C) advantage (D) Godliness

27. Provide one word for the underlined words.

Bhagat Singh, Raj guru and Batukeshwar Dutt were the patriots <u>of the same time.</u>

(A) Coherent (B) Contemporary
(C) Modern (D) Simultaneous

28. Find the odd one out in the given group of words.

Addition, supplement, companion, complement, accessory, adjunct, trimming, duplicate, accompaniment.

(A) Supplement (B) Duplicate
(C) Complement (D) Accessory

29. Find the correct spelling of a post in the Indian Army.

(A) Lefinant (B) Liutenant
(C) Lieutenant (D) Leutenant

30. Find the antonym of 'notorious'.

(A) Shameful (B) Moral
(C) Disreputable (D) Patent

31. Find the synonym of 'vindictive'.

(A) Vengeful (B) old timers
(C) vintage (D) forgiving

Read the passage carefully and answer the questions that follow:

The Ozone Layer

It's becoming very dangerous to sit in the sun. If you have a fashionable suntan, it doesn't necessarily mean that you have lots of outdoor activities – but it does mean that you're in greater danger of getting skin cancer and cataracts.

The ozone layer, which protects us from the sun's dangerous ultraviolet rays, is progressively deteriorating. In February 1992, a scientific report said that people in Canada, Northern Europe and Russia were in serious danger.

In 1985, the news of the destruction of the ozone layer in the South Pole alarmed people in the Southern Hemisphere. In Australia, there are now three times more cases of skin cancer than in the past. In New Zealand, teachers tell school children to wear hats and not to sit in the sun. What causes the destruction of the ozone layer? Mostly chlorofluorocarbons (CFCs), Aerosol sprays, refrigerators, air conditioners, as well as industrial chemicals, send chlorofluorocarbons into the atmosphere.

Governments are now trying very hard to forbid CFCs, but it will be expensive and difficult to do so. Alter the first ozone alarm in the Southern Hemisphere, ecologists all over the world asked governments to take strict measures immediately. Some governments did, but not soon enough. Other countries believe that they have other problems which are more important. Now stricter measures are going to be taken, but already a lot of damage has been done.

32. Ozone layer protects us from harmful ________.
    (A) gamma rays (B) ultraviolet rays
    (C) sun rays (D) None of these
33. Name the causative agent responsible for the destruction of ozone layer.
    (A) carcinogens
    (B) nitrogen containing compound
    (C) CFCs
    (D) None of these
34. Find the opposite of the word 'deteriorate'.
    (A) malfunction (B) to improve
    (C) worst (D) None of these
35. CFCs are caused by ________
    (A) Aerosol sprays, refrigerators, air conditioners
    (B) governments
    (C) ultraviolet rays
    (D) None of these

Read the given passage and answer the following questions.

The Reserve Bank of India (RBI) has come out with its annual report giving a balance-sheet of demonetisation implemented 21 months ago. Of Rs 15.41 lakh crore demonetised currency notes of Rs 500 and Rs 1,000 denominations, only Rs 10,720 crore did not reach to the banks or the RBI. This means only 0.7 per cent of demonetised currency notes were junked in the exercise. The government had initially expected that approximately Rs 3 lakh crore of demonetised currency notes would not come back to the banking system, thus shedding the substantial weight of black money.While announcing demonetisation on November 8 in 2016, Prime Minister Narendra Modi had outlined three broad objectives to fight black money, corruption and terror funding. These objectives have always been debatable for the lack of accurate verifiable data.

36. According to RBI report, what amount of money is not reached to RBI?
(A) Rs 10, 720 crore
(B) Rs 15.41 lakh crore
(C) Rs 3 lakh crore
(D) Rs 15, 840 crore

37. When did Prime Minister Narendra Modi announce demonetisation?
(A) October 8, 2016
(B) November 8, 2016
(C) November 8, 2017
(D) October 8, 2017

38. What was the main objectives of Prime Minister behind demonetisation?
(A) Poverty, black money, corruption
(B) Black money, corruption and terror funding
(C) Unemployment, Poverty, Black money
(D) Poverty, corruption, unemployment

SPOKEN AND WRITTEN EXPRESSIONS

39. Complete the most suitable option to complete the conversation.
Rohan: "Let's go out for long drive."
Anusha: "__________"
(A) No, it's so boring.
(B) Yes, Good idea!
(C) Can I take my another friend?
(D) None of these

40. Choose the correct option.
On Monday morning, there's always heavy traffic on all metro _______.
(A) means (B) ways
(C) routes (D) None of these

41. Put the sentences of the following conversation among two friends in order.
(a) Mayank: Life's rather tough. I desperately need a job.
(b) Tony: How much experience do you have in Accounts field?
(c) Tony : Hi, Mayank, how are you?
(d) Tony: We have a vacancy in our office for the post of an Accounts officer.
(e) Mayank: I have six years' experience in a reputed organisation as an Accounts officer.
(A) e, b, d, a, c (B) b, c, d, a, e
(C) c, a, d, b, e (D) a, e, d, b, c

42. Choose the best option.
Student: Thanks for your guidance, sir.
Teacher: _____________.
(A) I know you are thankful.
(B) You're welcome. I am pleased to help you.
(C) You should always be thankful.
(D) None of these

43. Choose the correct option.
Geeta: I'll be back in 5 minutes. Could you ________ care of my belongings, please?
Meena: Oh, Sure. Don't worry.
(A) save (B) take
(C) make (D) None of these

44. Choose the correct option.
Are your mom and dad still here?
(A) They are fine.
(B) We are a complete family.
(C) It' OK. Thanks.
(D) Yes, they are.

45. Choose the correct option.
Shikha: 'Hello'
Varsha: 'Could I speak to Mr. Batra?
Shikha: '___________. Can I take your message?
(A) In case it is urgent
(B) If you don't mind
(C) I'm afraid he is not at home.
(D) None of these

ACHIEVERS SECTION

46. Read the following conversation and complete the sentence given below.

Patient : Can I have an appointment with the doctor this evening? I am very sick.
Receptionist : I'm sorry. There's a long waiting list. You will have to wait for at least two weeks.

A patient went to his doctor's clinic and asked the receptionist _________ with the doctor that evening.

(A) if he can have an appointment.
(B) whether he could have an appointment
(C) that he can get an appointment.
(D) for an appointment.

47. Change the voice of the sentence.
The Kangaroo carried her baby in her pouch.

(A) The baby is carried by kangaroo in her pouch.
(B) The baby was carried by the kangaroo in her pouch.
(C) The kangaroo is carrying her baby in her pouch.
(D) None of these

48. Complete the sentence with suitable adverb.
I kept my car keys _______. I can't find it now.

(A) somewhere (B) everywhere
(C) here (D) there

49. Choose the most suitable one word substitution for the given description:

One who does a thing for pleasure and not as a profession.

(A) Immature (B) Auditor
(C) Amateur (D) None of these

50. Choose the correct synonym of the given word 'Fragile'.

(A) Defective (B) Hard
(C) Delicate (D) Deprived

Mock Test Paper 2

I E O

INTERNATIONAL ENGLISH OLYMPIAD

Total Questions : 50 Time : 1 Hour

PATTERN AND MARKING SCHEME				
Section	(1) Word and Structure Knowledge	(2) Reading	(3) Spoken and Written Expression	(4)Achievers
No. of Questions		45		5
Marks per Questions		1		3

SYLLABUS

Section – 1 : Synonyms, Antonyms, Analogies and Spellings, One Word, Word Order, Nouns, Pronouns, Verbs, Adverbs, Adjectives, Articles, Prepositions, Conjunctions, Punctuations, Jumbled Words, Voices, Concord, Question Forms, Tenses, Conditionals, Modals, Reported Speech. Collocations, Phrasal Verbs, Idioms, Homonyms and Homophones, Words related to Social Cause, Travel, Workplace, etc.

Section – 2 : Search for and retrieve information from various text types like Flyers, Classifieds, Dictionaries, etc., Understand information presented in Instruction Manual Format, Message Format and others. Acquire broad understanding of and look for specific information in longer texts like Editorials, Essays, etc.

Section – 3 : Ability to understand situation-based variations in functions like Giving Advice, Stating Preferences, Discussing Probability, Making an Offer, etc.

Section – 4 : Higher Order Thinking Questions - Syllabus as per Sections 1, 2 and 3.

WORD AND STRUCTURE KNOWLEDGE

1. Find the synonym of 'Kin'.
   (A) Relatives (B) Family
   (C) Clan (D) All of these
2. Find the antonym of 'Futile.
   (A) Waste (B) Fruitful
   (C) Imagination (D) Fancy
3. Find the correct spelling.
   (A) Embellishment
   (B) Accompaniment
   (C) Immediately
   (D) All of these
4. Find the odd one pair from the group of the words.
   Overseas, abroad, foreign, unknown, unfamiliar, domestic, strange, alien, familiar.
   (A) Unfamiliar, unknown
   (B) Overseas, abroad
   (C) Domestic, familiar
   (D) Alien, strange
5. Provide one word for 'the coining or using of the new word.'
   (A) Metropolitan (B) Coined
   (C) Neologism (D) Vocabulary
6. Fill in the blank and make a complete proverb.
   A chain is no stronger that its ____
   (A) Weakest link (B) Strongest link
   (C) Mediocre link (D) First link
7. Complete the sentence with the help of suitable phrasal verb.
   Even at this age my grandfather walks so fast that I could hardly _____ him.
   (A) get ahead (B) catch up with
   (C) leave him (D) get into

8. Fill in the blank with a collective noun.

Shikha is a very _____ orientated lady. She left her job for the family.

(A) Colleague (B) Family
(C) Daughter (D) Society

9. Complete the sentence with insertion of suitable pronouns.

Jay and Veeru were riding ___ bicycles. For their fun they bumped into each other knowingly and hurt _____.

(A) your, yourself (B) our, ourselves
(C) my, myself (D) their, themselves

10. Place the given words in a meaningful sequence.

harmless human animal are to beings most

(A) human beings are harmless to many animals
(B) harmless are many animals to human being
(C) most animals are harmless to human being
(D) to harmless human beings are most animals

11. Insert the suitable adverb of place in the following sentence.

Aditi has just gone _____. Tell her to get my medicine while coming up.

(A) downstairs (B) upstairs
(C) downwards (D) upwards

12. Complete the sentence with most appropriate conjunction.

Kavya needs to work hard ____ she can pass her exam.

(A) so that (B) although
(C) or (D) but

13. Choose the suitable word for the statement given below.

"A preconceived opinion that one forms without any reason or actual experience."

(A) Intolerance (B) Prejudice
(C) Peer pressure (D) Racism

14. Choose the correct option.

Meera has been appointed for the post of _______ in a reputed organisation.

(A) Resume
(B) Management
(C) Human Resource
(D) hike

15. Choose the suitable word for the given description.

A long journey involving travel by sea or in space

(A) Snowbird (B) Caravan
(C) Voyage (D) Rover

16. Change the given direct speech into indirect.
Rohan said, 'I am very busy now'.

(A) Rohan said that he was very busy then.
(B) Rohan said that he is very busy now.
(C) Rohan said he is very busy then.
(D) Rohan said that he would be very busy now.

17. Choose the appropriate adjective for the underlined phrases in the sentence given below.

Arnav considers himself <u>much more important than other people</u> and self-congratulatory during his speech at an Annual General meeting of his company.

(A) affectionate (B) pompous
(C) witty (D) None of these

18. Choose the most appropriate prepositions from the given options.

The police caught the thief _________ the corner of Shivaji Park Street.

(A) for (B) on
(C) at (D) with

19. Complete the sentence with suitable form of the tense.

Suhani _____ teaching music at the academy for ten years.

(A) had (B) have been
(C) has been (D) is

20. Find the meaning of idiom 'To feel under the weather'.
(A) Something is very easy.
(B) To not feel well
(C) to accidentally reveal a secret.
(D) something that will never happen.

21. Choose the correct option.
Indian team had _____ the World Cup Match.
(A) one
(B) won
(C) Both (A) and (B)
(D) None of these

22. Change the given voice into passive one.
The children have broken the window pane.
(A) Both (B) and (C)
(B) The window pane have broken by the children.
(C) The window pane has been broken by the children.
(D) None of these

23. Choose the correct option to fill in the blank.
There are a lot of books in the library, _________?
(A) is there (B) aren't there
(C) are there (D) isn't there

24. Insert the correct concord in the sentence given below.
The girls _______ very happy as they had just won their dance competition.
(A) are (B) is
(C) have (D) None of these

25. Choose the correct option.
Seema wants to ________ her mistakes.
(A) apologize with (B) apologize to
(C) apologize for (D) None of these

26. Complete the conversation.
Mansi : Your dress is very pretty. Please tell me ___________.
Kavya : I bought it from a showroom which is situated at Lajpat Nagar.
(A) where you bought it from.
(B) why you bought it.
(C) when you bought it.
(D) where did you buy it from.

27. Choose the correct option.
We ______ prepare our lessons well before examination.
(A) has to (B) must
(C) ought to (D) have to

28. Arrange the jumbled words to form a meaningful sentence.
everywhere / and / is respected / honest man / an / admired.
(A) Everywhere an honest man admired and is respected.
(B) An honest man is respected and admired everywhere.
(C) Admired and is respected an honest man everywhere.
(D) None of these

29. Choose the correct punctuation for the given sentence.
This is absolutely wonderful _____.
(A) ! (B) .
(C) : (D) ;

30. Complete the sentence with suitable homonyms.
Dr. Batra has too many _______, it takes so long to get an appointment.
(A) patients
(B) patience
(C) Both (A) and (B)
(D) None of these

31. Fill in the blank with suitable article.
Riya and her family visited ______ Akshar Dhaam temple in June. There was __ fountain in the middle of the temple.
(A) The, a
(B) The, an
(C) The, No article
(D) None of these

Read the passage carefully and answer the following questions.

Alfred Hitchcock was a man with vivid imagination, strong creative skills and a passion for life. With his unique style and God-gifted wit he produced and directed some of the most thrilling films that had the audience almost swooning with fright and falling off their seats with laughter. Alfred Hitchcock was greatly influenced by American films and magazines. At the age of 20, he took up a job at the office of Paramount Studio, London. Using imagination, talent and dedication, he made each of his endeavours a success. He took great pleasure in working in the studio and often worked all seven days a week. He moved to the USA in 1939 and got his American citizenship in 1955. Here, he produced many more films and hosted a weekly television show. No matter from where his ideas came, whether a magazine article, a mystery novel or incident, his films had the typical "Hitchcock touch"-where the agony of suspense was relieved by interludes of laughter! Hitchcock was knighted in 1980.

32. Where did Alfred Hitchcock get a job at the age of 20?
    (A) Parasymphony Studio, London
    (B) Universal Studio, London
    (C) Paramount Studio, London
    (D) Mount studio, London

33. The typical Hitchcock style of film-making include ______
    (A) suspense and humour
    (B) romance and thriller
    (C) fear and suspense
    (D) None of these

34. What is Alfred Hitchcock famous as?
    (A) Dancer (B) Actor
    (C) Film Producer (D) writer

35. Find the opposite of the word 'endeavours'.
    (A) attempt (B) abandon
    (C) undertake (D) struggle

Read the given passage and answer the question from 36 to 38.

At a time when cancer is spreading at a disturbingly fast pace across the globe, an Israeli biotech company have claimed that they will have the cure for this deadly disease by 2020. Although different types of treatments are available in the market, but nothing promises to cure this deadly disease 100%. But Accelerated Evolution Biotechnologies Ltd (AEBi), founded in 2000 from the ITEK Weizmann technology incubator has made bold claims to cure the disease completely.

CEO of the biotech company Dr Ilan Morad said they started with identifying why other cancer-related drugs and treatment are not working and then they looked for an effective way to counter it. The treatment which the biotech company calls MuTaTo (multi-target toxin) is based on SoAP technology, which belongs to the phage display group of technologies.

Most cancer drugs attack a specific target or on the cancer cell, but MuTaTo attacks the cancer cell's receptors from three different directions. "Instead of attacking receptors one at a time, we attack receptors three at a time. Not even cancer can mutate three receptors at one time," said Morad, to the daily newspaper.

36. Who is the CEO of Accelerated Evolution Biotechnologies Ltd?
    (A) Dr. Ilan Morad
    (B) Dr. Khalid Abbed
    (C) Dr. Myles. B. Abbott
    (D) Dr. William A. Abdu

37. On which technology the treatment named MuTaTo is based?
(A) LSO crystal technology
(B) VMAT
(C) soAP technology
(D) C AR-T

38. How MuTaTo could be differ from other cancer treatments?
(A) It can cure the cancer in only days while other takes months
(B) Most cancer drugs attack the receptors from single direction but MuTaTo attacks from three different directions
(C) Most cancer drugs attack the receptors from single direction but MuTaTo attacks from two different directions.
(D) MuTaTo treatment of cancer takes much time to cure the cancer as compare to other treatments.

SPOKEN AND WRITTEN EXPRESSIONS

39. Choose the best option.
Monica: Papa, I've been selected the best student of the school.
Papa: ___________.
(A) Thank you. You are my topper.
(B) Well done! Congrats my daughter.
(C) you don't deserve it.
(D) None of these

40. Choose the correct option.
Kriti : There is an annual trade fair next week. ______ to go?
Krishan : This sounds like great fun. Let me ask my friends.
(A) Do you want (B) Shall we
(C) Would you (D) None of these

41. Put the sentences of the following conversation in proper order.
a. How could he do mathematical problems so fast?
b. Ishan completed his Maths worksheet very quickly.
c. But his calculations were accurate.
d. He has done abacus classes for many years.
(A) c, b, a, d (B) a, d, c, b
(C) b, c, a, d (D) a, c, d, b

42. Fill in the blank with suitable option.
You can borrow my Science notes, but please ______ good care of it.
(A) made (B) take
(C) has (D) None of these

43. Complete the conversation.
Aakash: Excuse me, I think my vehicle requires fuel. Could you tell me the way to the nearest petrol pump?
Abhinav: I can show you. I'm going that way.
(A) Please go ahead. I am getting late.
(B) I am so lucky to meet you
(C) Really? That's very kind of you
(D) None of these

44. Choose the correct option.
Manager: Should you require any help, please _______.
Customer: Sure, thanks.
(A) have patience (B) answer me
(C) feel free to ask (D) None of these

45. Choose the correct option to complete the dialogue.
Mansi : Anshika, it's the Accounts class now! I forgot my book.
(A) Could you lend me your accounts notebook, please?
(B) Can I got an Accounts book?
(C) Could you share your book with me today?
(D) None of these

ACHIEVERS SECTION

46. Choose the correct option to complete the sentence.

    The farmers ________ their fields since 9 O' clock.

    (A) has been ploughed
    (B) have been ploughing
    (C) have ploughed
    (D) were ploughed

47. Insert the suitable preposition.

    The teacher asked Manav to tell the name of the students who were responsible _____ that misbehaviour.

    (A) with (B) for
    (C) on (D) at

48. Choose the correct option for the meaning of the given idiom.

    "Judge a book by its cover"

    (A) Rely on inward appearances
    (B) Rely on misconception
    (C) Rely on outward appearances
    (D) None of these

49. Change the speech of the sentence.

    The teacher said to the students, "Listen to me attentively."

    (A) The teacher said to the students that listen to her attentively.
    (B) The teacher asked the students to listen to him attentively.
    (C) The teacher told the students to listen to me attentively.
    (D) None of these

50. Choose the correct option to complete the conversation.

    Sonam : Do you think we will be able to complete the assignment in time?

    Aakriti : ____________.

    (A) I don't so think
    (B) I don't think so
    (C) I do so think
    (D) None of these

Hints and Solutions

INTERNATIONAL MATHEMATICS OLYMPIAD (IMO)

MOCK TEST PAPER – 1

ANSWERS									
1. (C)	2. (D)	3. (C)	4. (C)	5. (B)	6. (A)	7. (B)	8. (C)	9. (A)	10. (C)
11. (B)	12. (C)	13. (B)	14. (B)	15. (D)	16. (A)	17. (C)	18. (C)	19. (C)	20. (C)
21. (B)	22. (B)	23. (A)	24. (C)	25. (C)	26. (D)	27. (B)	28. (C)	29. (C)	30. (B)
31. (B)	32. (C)	33. (C)	34. (B)	35. (B)	36. (A)	37. (D)	38. (A)	39. (B)	40. (A)
41. (B)	42. (B)	43. (D)	44. (C)	45. (D)	46. (C)	47. (B)	48. (B)	49. (C)	50. (A)

1. (C) New sequence of letters
E L B I S S [O] P M I

2. (D) Given expression = $(10 \times 3) \div (14 - 4) + (19 + 9) = 31$

3. (C) Heights in ascending order:
$R < P < Q < T$ and $R < S < Q$
i.e., $R < P < S < Q < T$
or $R < S < P < Q < T$

4. (C) Each letter in the word is moved one step backward to obtain the corresponding letter of the code. Hence, DISPOSE is written as CHRONRD.

5. (B)

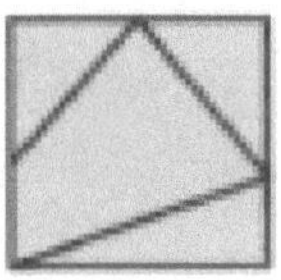

6. (A)

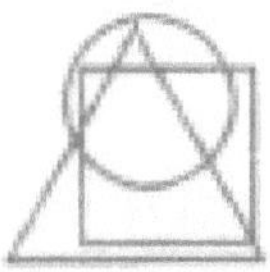

7. (B) If we turn figure (i) in such a way that the positions of its nos. 2 and 3 are as in figure (ii), then 5 will reach to bottom. So, 5 and 6 are opposite to each other.

8. (C) Unfolded form of the given figure (X)

9. (A)

10. (C)

11. (B) Mirror Image of given figure:

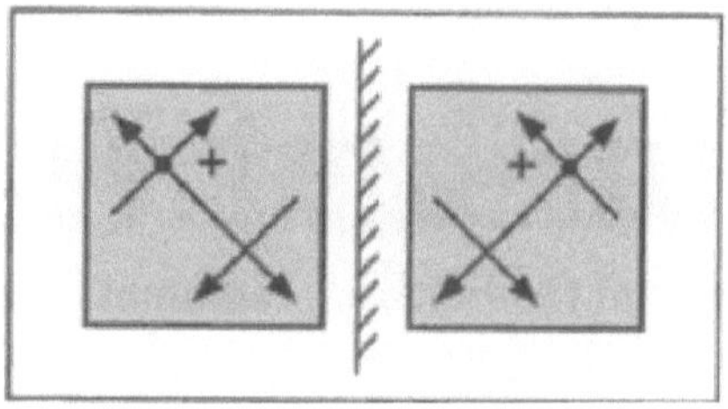

13. (B) Three black points and two black points appear alternately. Every time one small horizontal line is increasing in the figure.

14. (B) The white and the black leaves rotate in anticlockwise direction by 90° and 135° respectively.

15. (D) All the three circles are in a straight line only in figure (D).

16. (A) Probability is 5/15 = 1/3

17. (C)

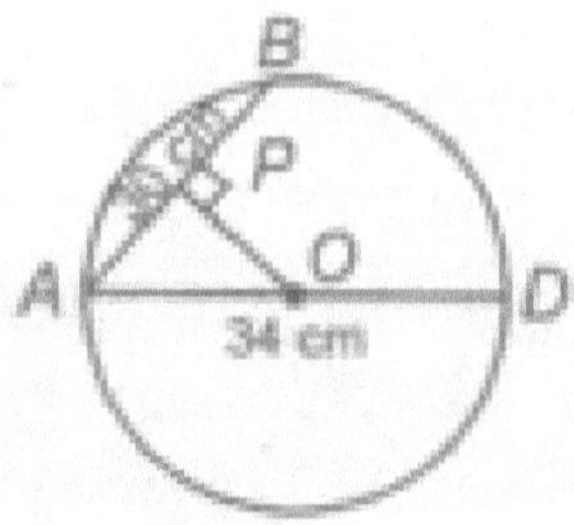

Radius = 17 cm, AP = 15 cm
$\angle APO = 90°$
By Pythagoras theorem
$(OP)^2 = (17)^2 - (15)^2 = 289 - 225 = 64$
OP = 8 cm

18. (C) Area of || gm = Base × Height
$= 12 \times 10 = 120 \text{ cm}^2$
Area of || gm = CD × 8
120 = CD × 8
CD = 120 ÷ 8 = 15 cm

19. (C) In quadrilateral ABCD,
$\angle A + \angle B + \angle C + \angle D = 360°$
$\angle A + \angle B = 360° - 2(\angle 1 + \angle 2)$ ...(i)
In ΔDEC
$\angle CED + \angle 1 + \angle 2 = 180°$ (sum of angles of a triangle)
$\angle 1 + \angle 2 = 180° - \angle CED$ ....(ii)
Put the value in (i)
$\angle A + \angle B = 360° - 2(180° - \angle CED)$
$\angle A + \angle B = 2\angle CED$

20. (C) Let $f(x) = x^3 - 2x^2 + px - q$
and $g(x) = x^2 - 2x - 3$
$= (x-3)(x+1)$
Now when $g(x)$ divides $f(x)$, it leaves a remainder $(x - 6)$.
Then, we have, $f(3) = x - 6$ and $f(-1) = x - 6$
$\Rightarrow 27 - 18 + 3p - q$
$= 3 - 6$ and $-1 - 2 - p - q$
$= -1 - 6$
$\Rightarrow 3p - q = -12$ ...(i)
and $p + q = 4$ ...(ii)
On adding (i) and (ii)
$4p = -8 \Rightarrow p = -2$ and
$q = 3(-2) + 12 = -6 + 12 = 6$

21. (B) By Pythagoras theorem,
$PQ^2 = 256 + 144 = 400$
PQ = 20 cm
Semi- perimeter = 52 + 48 + 20/2
= 120/2 = 60 cm
Area of ΔPQR
$= \sqrt{60(60-52)(60-48)(60-20)}$
Area of ΔPQR
$= \sqrt{60 \times 8 \times 12 \times 40}$
Area of ΔPQR
$= \sqrt{10 \times 10 \times 6 \times 6 \times 2 \times 2 \times 2 \times 2 \times 4}$
Area of ΔPQR
$= 10 \times 6 \times 4 \times 2 = 480 \text{ cm}^2$

22. (B) We have,
$\Rightarrow 2^x 2^{-3} \cdot 3^{2x} 3^{-8} = 36$
$\Rightarrow 2^x \cdot \frac{1}{2^3} \cdot 3^x \cdot 3^x \cdot \frac{1}{3^8} = 36$
$\Rightarrow (2 \times 3 \times 3)^x = 36 \times 8 \times 6561$
$\Rightarrow (18)^x = (18)^5$

23. (A) $x + 35° = 65°$

$x = 30°$

24. (C) We have,

$\sqrt[4]{(81)^{-2}}$

$= (9)^{-4\times\frac{1}{4}} = 9$

25. (C) Side of rhombus = 10 cm

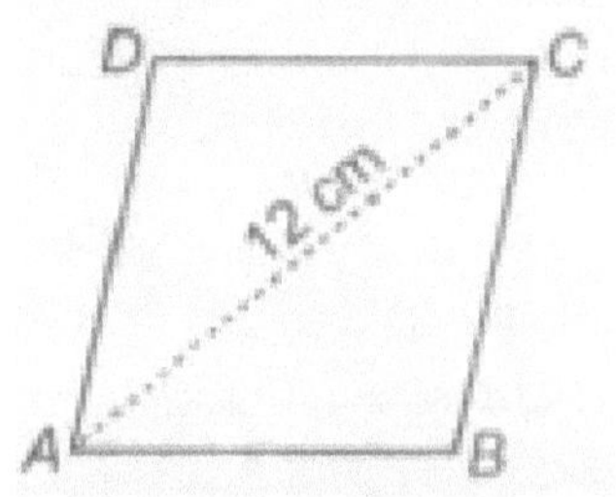

$a = 10$ cm, $b = 12$ cm, $c = 10$ cm

By Heron's formula

Now, semi-perimeter of ΔABC is

$= \frac{a+b+c}{2}$

$= \left(\frac{10+10+12}{2}\right)$ cm

$= \frac{32}{2}$ cm $= 16$ cm

$\therefore$ Area of ΔABC

$= \sqrt{16(16-10)(16-10)(16-12)}\ \text{cm}^2$

$= \sqrt{16\times6\times6\times4}\ \text{cm}^2 = 48\ \text{cm}^2$

Area to be painted = 96 cm^2

Cost of painting = 5 × 96 = ₹ 480

Cost of painting the sheet on both the sides = 480 + 480 = ₹ 960

26. (D) Ratio of their volumes

$\frac{\pi r_1^2 h_1}{\pi r_2^2 h_2} = \frac{4\times5}{9\times3} = 20:27$

27. (B) We have,

$\frac{1}{3}\times(15)^{27} = \frac{15\times(15)^{26}}{3}$

$= 5\times(15)^{26}$

28. (C) Co- ordinates of point R is (4, 4)

29. (C) Put $x = 2$ and $y = 0$ in the given equation

$2x + 3y = k$

$4 + 0 = k$

$k = 4$

30. (B) $12x + 8 + 8x - 3 + 55 = 180°$ (sum of angles)

$20x = 180° - 60°$

$x = 6°$

31. (B) We have,

PR = QS

$\Rightarrow PR - QR = QS - QR \Rightarrow PQ = RS$

32. (C) AE = AD, BD = CE (Given)

$\Rightarrow$ AE + CE = AD + BD

AC = AB ...(i)

In ΔAEB and ΔADC,

AE = AD

∠EAB = ∠DAC [Common]

AC = AB [From (i)]

$\therefore$ ΔAEB ≅ ΔADC

[SAS congurency rule]

33. (C) Volume of the metal sheet

= (27 × 8 × 1) = 216 cm^2

Surface area of the metal sheet

= 2(27 × 8 + 8 × 1 + 1 × 27)

− 2(216 + 8 + 27) − 502 cm^2

Volume of cube = Volume of metal sheet

(side)^3 = 216 cm^3 $\Rightarrow$ side

= 6 cm

Now, surface area of cube

$= 6(6)^2 = 216\ \text{cm}^2$

$\therefore$ Required difference

$= (502 - 216)\ \text{cm}^2 = 286\ \text{cm}^2$

34. (B) Let ABCD be the trapezium with sides AB = 25 cm, CD = 10 cm, AD = 14 cm, BC = 13 cm.

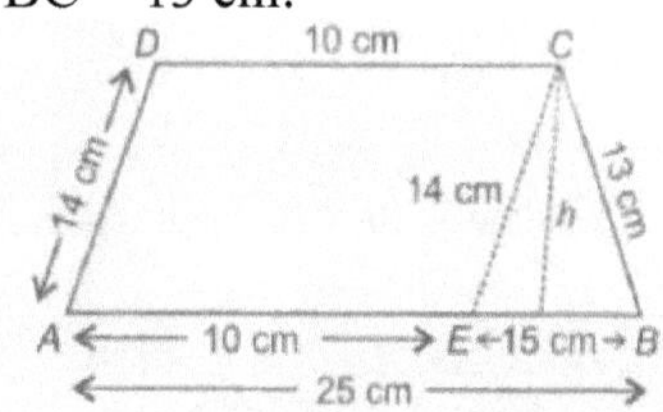

Draw CE || AD

Area of trapezium ABCD = Area of || gm AECD + Area of Δ ECB

Now, in Δ ECB

$$s = \frac{14+13+15}{2} = 21$$

∴ Area of ΔECB

$$= \sqrt{21(21-14)(21-13)(21-15)}$$

$$= 84 \text{ cm}^2$$

Also, area of ΔEBC

$$= \frac{1}{2} \times BE \times h \Rightarrow \frac{1}{2} \times 15 \times h = 84$$

$$\therefore h = 11.2 \text{ cm}$$

∴ Area of parallelogram AECD

$$= \text{AE} \times \text{h} = 10 \times 11.2 = 112 \text{ cm}^2$$

Hence, area of trapezium

$= 112 + 84 = 196 \text{ cm}^2$

35. (B) Sum of observations = 50 × 100 = 5000
Correct sum = 5000 + 150 – 50 = 5100
New mean = 5100/100 = 51

36. (A) Average = Sum of scores in all subjects/ No. of subjects

$$\Rightarrow 60 = \frac{63+57+82+55+x}{5}$$

$$\Rightarrow 257 + x = 300 \Rightarrow x = 43$$

Marks scored in five subjects are 63, 57, 82, 55, 43.
∴ Best four marks are 63, 57, 82, 55.
∴ Required average

$$= \frac{63+57+82+55}{4} = 64.25$$

37. (D) Semi-perimeter = 90 m
Area of field

$$= \sqrt{90 \times 40 \times 25 \times 25} = 1500$$

Cost of laying grass
= 1500 × 7 = ₹ 10500

38. (A) Let length = x m
B = 40 – x m
Original area = $x(40 - x)$ m^2
New length = $x - 2$,
New breadth = $42 - x$
New area = $(x - 2)(42 - x)$
According to question
$(x - 2)(42 - x) - x(40 - x) = 16$
$x = 25$
Length = 25 m, breadth = 40 – 25 = 15 m

39. (B) Let radius = r
Original area = πr^2
New radius = $r/2$

$$\text{New area} = \pi\left(\frac{r}{2}\right)^2$$

Difference = $3\pi r^2/4$
% decrease = 75%

40. (A) According to question,
$2\times$ cost of pen = Cost of notebook

$$\Rightarrow 2y = x \Rightarrow x - 2y = 0$$

41. (B) Let original SP = ₹ x
New selling price = 2/3 of x
Loss = 10%

$$CP = \left[\frac{100}{90} \times \frac{2}{3}x\right] = \frac{20}{27}x$$

Gain = $7x/27$
Gain% = 35%

42. (B) Side of an equilateral triangle = 12 cm

$$\text{Area} = \frac{\sqrt{3}}{4}a^2$$

$$= \frac{\sqrt{3}}{4} \times 12 \times 12$$

$$= 36\sqrt{3} \text{ cm}^2$$

43. (D) Money she has = ₹ $(x^3 - 3x^2 + 4x + 50)$
Cost of each chocolate = ₹ $(x - 3)$

$$\begin{array}{r|l} & x^2 + 4 \\ \hline x - 3 & x^3 - 3x^2 + 4x + 50 \\ & x^3 - 3x^2 \\ & - \quad + \\ \hline & \quad 4x + 50 \\ & \quad 4x - 12 \\ & \quad - \quad + \\ \hline & \quad\quad 62 \end{array}$$

$$\therefore x^3 - 3x^2 + 4x + 50 = (x-3)\left(x^2+4\right) + 62$$

So, Shivani buys $(x^2 + 4)$ chocolates

and ₹ 62 left with her.

44. (C) Total balls played by him = 20
Boundary hit by ball = 15 times
Probability = 5/20 = 1/4

45. (D) No. of bricks = Volume of wall/Volume of each brick
No. of bricks = 10800000/1687.5
= 6400

46. (C) Join BD.

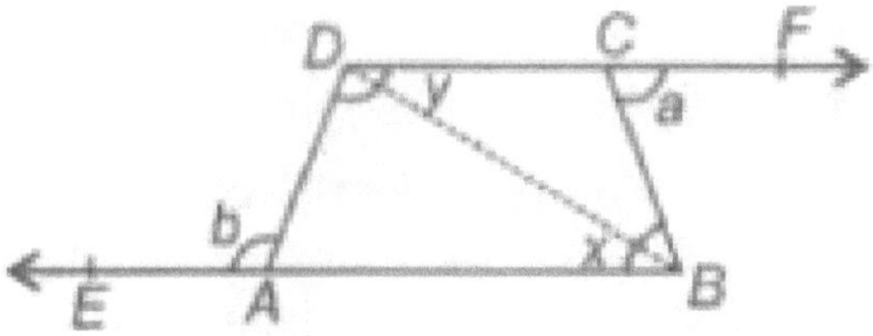

In ΔABD, we have
$\angle ABD + \angle ADB = b$ ... (i)

In ΔCBD, we have
$\angle CBD + \angle CDB = a$ ...(ii)

Adding (i) and (ii) we get
$(\angle ABD + \angle CBD) + (\angle ADB + \angle CDB)$
$= a + b$
$\Rightarrow x + y = a + b$

47. (B) By using Pythagoras theorem
AC = 41 cm

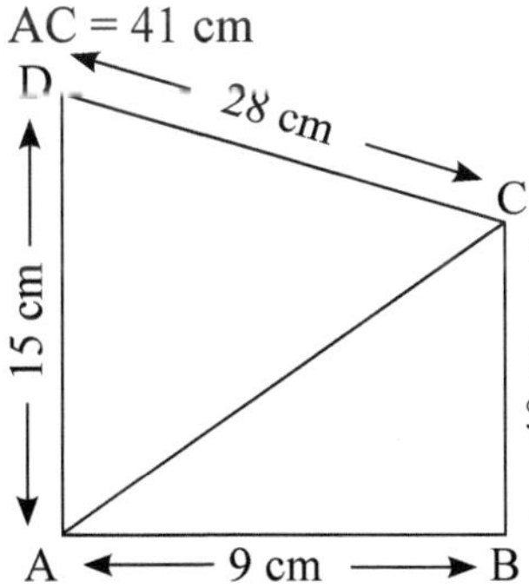

$\therefore$ Area of ΔABC

$= \frac{1}{2} \times 9 \times 40 = 180 \text{ cm}^2$

Now in Δ ADC

$s = \frac{15 + 28 + 41}{2} = 42 \text{ cm}$

$\therefore$ Area of ΔADC

$= \sqrt{42 \times 27 \times 14 \times 1} = 126 \text{ cm}^2$

Hence, area of quadrilateral ABCD
= (180 + 126) cm^2 = 306 cm^2

48. (B) ∠ADB = 90° [Angle in semi -circle]
Now, in
$\Delta ADB, \angle DAB + \angle ADB + \angle ABD = 180°$
$30° + 90° + \angle ABD = 180° \Rightarrow \angle ABD = 60°$

In cyclic quadrilateral ABDC, we have
∠ABD + ∠ACD = 180°
⇒ 60° + ∠ACD = 180°
⇒ ∠ACD = 120°
Also, ∠CDA = 30° = ∠DAB
In ΔCAD, ∠CAD + ∠CDA + ∠ACD = 180°

⇒ ∠CAD + 30° + 120° = 180°
∠CAD = 30°

49. (C) The level of water rises by 6.75 cm.
$\therefore$ Volume increased in the cylindrical part
$\pi r^2 h = \pi \times 12 \times 12 \times 6.75 \text{ cm}^3$
Thus, the volume of the spherical ball
$= \pi \times 12 \times 12 \times 6.75 \text{ cm}^3$

Let R be the radius of the spherical ball.

$\therefore$ Volume of spherical ball $= \frac{4}{3}\pi R^3$

Now, $\frac{4}{3}\pi R^3 = \pi \times 12 \times 12 \times 6.75$

$\Rightarrow R^3 = \frac{3 \times 12 \times 12 \times 6.75}{4} \Rightarrow R^3 = 729$

$\Rightarrow R = 9$

Hence, radius of the sphere = 9 cm

50. (A)

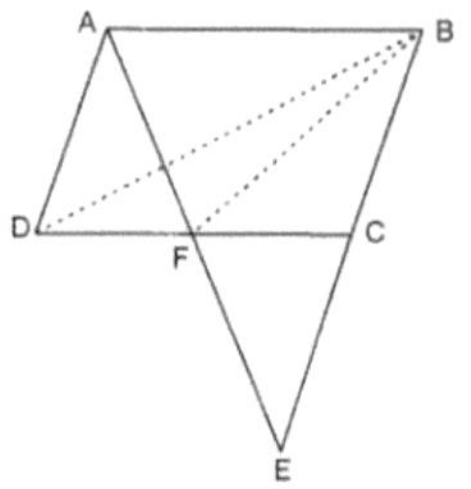

In ΔADF and ΔECF , we have

$\angle ADF = \angle ECF$ [alt. int. $\angle$s]

$AD = EC$ [$\because AD = BC$ and $BC = EC$]

$\angle DFA = \angle CFE$ [vert. opp. $\angle$s]

$\therefore$ By AAS congruence rule ,

$\Delta ADF \cong \Delta ECF$

$\Rightarrow DF = CF$ [c.p.c.t.]

$\Rightarrow$ ar (ΔADF) = ar (ΔECF)

Now, $DF = CF$

$\Rightarrow$ BF is a median in ΔBDC

$\Rightarrow$ ar(ΔBDC) = 2 ar(ΔDFB)

$= 2 \times 3 = 6$ cm^2 [$\because$ar(ΔDFB) = 3 cm^2]

Thus, ar(||gm ABCD) = 2 ar(ΔBDC)

$= 2 \times 6 = 12$ cm^2

MOCK TEST PAPER – 2

ANSWERS									
1. (D)	2. (B)	3. (D)	4. (C)	5. (C)	6. (C)	7. (B)	8. (C)	9. (B)	10. (C)
11. (A)	12. (B)	13. (B)	14. (C)	15. (B)	16. (C)	17. (A)	18. (A)	19. (C)	20. (A)
21. (B)	22. (D)	23. (A)	24. (B)	25. (C)	26. (D)	27. (C)	28. (C)	29. (A)	30. (B)
31. (C)	32. (B)	33. (C)	34. (C)	35. (C)	36. (A)	37. (B)	38. (A)	39. (C)	40. (B)
41. (B)	42. (A)	43. (D)	44. (B)	45. (C)	46. (C)	47. (A)	48. (C)	49. (C)	50. (B)

1. (D) In each pair, the second number is the cube of the first number as shownbelow. Hence, (7 – 341) is different from others.

2. (B) No. of married women who are unemployed and non-vegetarians is 40.

3. (D) Kalpana started her journey from the point A and finished also at the same point A.

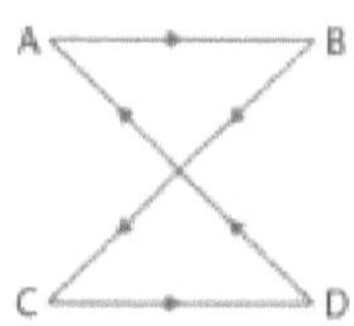

4. (C) $P - M \rightarrow$ P is the brother of M

$M + N \rightarrow$ M is the mother of N

$N \times Q \rightarrow$ N is the sister of Q

Therefore, P is the maternal uncle of Q.

5. (B) A man wears hat on his head but head means knee.

6. (C)

7. (B) No. of cubes in the figure is 89.

8. (C) The circles in each row occur with two, three and four bars.

9. (B)

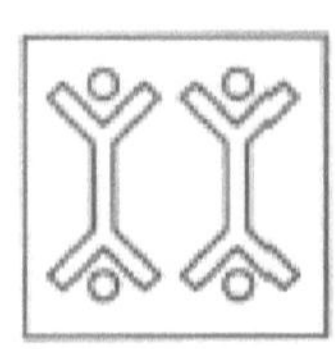

10. (C)

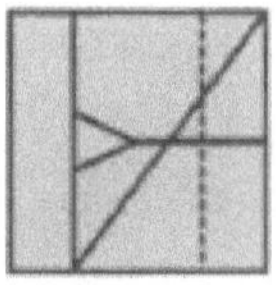

11. (A) Mirror image

12. (B) Water image of the given figure

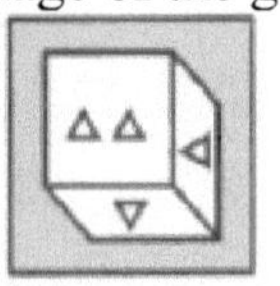

13. (B) No. of rectangles is 18.

14. (C) The figure gets vertically inverted with a similar figure in it.

15. (B) The pin moves 1, 2, 3, 4, 5,...., spaces clockwise sequentially. The arrow moves two steps anticlockwise in each step.

16. (C) No. of terms = 10, which is even.

$\therefore$ Median = average of $\left(\frac{10}{2}\right)^{th}$ term and

$\left(\frac{10}{2}+1\right)^{th}$ term

$\Rightarrow$ Median = average of 5th and 6th terms

$\Rightarrow 63=\frac{1}{2}(x+x+2) \Rightarrow x+1$

$=63 \Rightarrow x=62$

17. (A) No. of planks = Volume of pit/ Volume of each plank

$=\frac{16\times12\times4}{4\times0.50\times0.20}=1920$

18. (A) Perimeter = 32 cm

Let one of the equal sides be $3x$ and other be $2x$.

$\therefore 3x+3x+2x=32$

$\Rightarrow 8x=32 \Rightarrow x=4$

Sides of isosceles triangle = 12 cm, 12 cm, 8 cm

$\therefore s=\frac{32}{2}=16\text{cm}$

Area $=\sqrt{16\times4\times4\times8}=32\sqrt{2}\text{ cm}^2$

19. (C) Given: $\angle BDC = 42°$

Since, angles in the same segment are equal.

$\therefore \angle BAC = \angle BDC = 42°$

20. (A) AC = BD (given)

$\Rightarrow AC-BC=BD-BC \Rightarrow AB=CD$

21. (B) The point M has y -coordinate = 10 or –10

22. (D) Let $f(x) = 3x^2 + 8x^2 - 6x + 1$

It is given that $f(x)$ is divided by $x + 3$.

Put $x = -3$ in the given expression

Now, $f(-3)$

$=3(-3)^3+8(-3)^2-6(-3)+1$

$=-81+72+18+1=10$

23. (A) Perimeter of a circle = Perimeter of a square

$2\pi r=4a$

$2\times\frac{22}{7}\times r=4a$

$r=\frac{7a}{11}$

Area of circle = $14\ a^2/11$

Area of square = a^2

Ratio = $14\ a^2/11 : a^2 = 14 : 11$

24. (B) Let mother's age = x years

Person's age = 2/5 of x

According to question

$\frac{1}{2}(x+8)=2/5 \text{ of } x+8$

$\frac{x+8}{2}=\frac{2}{5}x+8$

$x=40$

25. (C) No. of cubes = Volume of a cube/ Volume of a small cubes

No. of cubes = 64000/512 = 125

26. (D) We have,

$$49x^2 - b = \left(7x + \frac{1}{2}\right)\left(7x - \frac{1}{2}\right)$$

$$49x^2 - b = 49x^2 - \frac{1}{4}$$

On comparing both the sides

$b = 1/4$

27. (C) Volume of a cone = $1/3\pi r^2 h$

Volume of a cone = 38.808 cm^3

Volume of a sphere = $4/3\ \pi r^3$

Radius of the sphere = 2.1 cm

28. (C) Length of DC or $x = 3 + 7 + 3 = 13$ cm

29. (A) We have,

$$m = \frac{\sqrt{3}+\sqrt{2}}{\sqrt{3}-\sqrt{2}} \text{ and } n = \frac{\sqrt{3}-\sqrt{2}}{\sqrt{3}+\sqrt{2}}$$

$$m^2 + n^2 = \left(\frac{\sqrt{3}+\sqrt{2}}{\sqrt{3}-\sqrt{2}}\right)^2 + \left(\frac{\sqrt{3}-\sqrt{2}}{\sqrt{3}+\sqrt{2}}\right)^2$$

$$m^2 + n^2 = \frac{5+2\sqrt{6}}{5-2\sqrt{6}} + \frac{5-2\sqrt{6}}{5+2\sqrt{6}}$$

$$m^2 + n^2 = 98$$

30. (B) $x - y = 0$ is not the equation of one of the boundary lines.

31. (C) As diagonals of rhombus bisect the angles.

$\therefore \angle BAC = \angle CAD$

Also, in rhombus ABCD,

$\angle$A + $\angle$B = 180° (sum of adjacent angles)

$$\Rightarrow \angle A + 56^\circ = 180^\circ \Rightarrow \angle A = 124^\circ$$

$$\therefore \angle BAC = \angle CAD = \frac{\angle A}{2} = 62^\circ$$

Now $\angle ACD = \angle BAC$

[alternate angles]

$\Rightarrow \angle ACD = \angle BAC$

32. (B) AB || CD

$x = 360° - (40° + 35°)$

$x = 360° - 75°$

$x = 285°$

33. (C) In the given figure

AD = AD (Common)

$\angle$BAD = $\angle$CAD

AB = AC

Hence, both triangles are congruent to each other by SAS rule.

34. (C) D, E, F are mid-points of sides BC, AC, AB.

Then, ar (ΔABC)

$= $ ar $[\Delta AFE + \Delta FED + \Delta EDC + FBD]$

Also, ar $\Delta AFE =$ ar ΔFED

$=$ ar $\Delta EDC =$ ar ΔFBD

$$\Rightarrow \text{ar}(\Delta AFE) = \frac{\text{ar}(\Delta ABC)}{4}$$

$$= \frac{28}{4} = 7\text{cm}^2$$

Now, Area of parallelogram AEDF

$= \text{ar}(\Delta AEF + \Delta EFD)$

$= (7 + 7)\ \text{cm}^2 = 14\ \text{cm}^2$

35. (C) Total number of cards = 52

Number of cards that are neither red nor a queen= 52 − 26 − 2 = 24

Required probability = 24/52 = 6/13

36. (A) Circumference = 440 cm

$r = 70$ cm

Volume of iron = External volume − Internal volume

Volume of iron

$= \pi r_1^2 h - \pi r_2^2 h$

$= \pi(70^2 - 66^2) \times 63$

$$= \frac{22}{7} \times 136 \times 4 \times 63 = 107712\ \text{cm}^3$$

37. (B) Total balls = 40

No. of white balls = 5

Probability = 5/40 = 1/8

38. (A) Semi- perimeter = 54

Area of triangular ground

$= \sqrt{54(54-51)(54-37)(54-20)}$

$= \sqrt{54 \times 3 \times 17 \times 34}$

$= \sqrt{9 \times 6 \times 3 \times 17 \times 17 \times 2} = 306\ \text{m}^2$

Cost of levelling = 306 × 3 = ₹ 918

39. (C) MP = ₹ 625

$$SP = \left[\frac{75}{100}\right] \times 625 = 468.75$$

CP = 500

Loss = 31.25

Loss% = 31.25/500 × 100 = 6.25%

40. (B) Volume of the tank

$= \left(x^4 - 81y^4\right)\text{m}^3$

41. (B) Semi–perimeter = 12 cm

Area of triangular cardboard

$= \sqrt{12(12-6)(12-8)(12-10)}$

$= \sqrt{12 \times 6 \times 4 \times 2} = 24 \text{ m}^2$

Cost of painting = 24 × .09 = ₹ 2.16

42. (A) Let sum be ₹ x.

$CI = A - P$

$$525 = x\left[1 + \frac{10}{100}\right]^2 - x$$

$$525 = \frac{121}{100}x - x$$

$x = 2500$

SI = PRT/100 = ₹ 500

43. (D) Radius = 7 m

Height = 24 m

∴ Now slant height of the cone,

$l = \sqrt{h^2 + r^2}$

$= \sqrt{(24)^2 + (7)^2} = \sqrt{576 + 49} = \sqrt{625}$

$l = 25$ m

Curved surface area of conical tent

$= \pi rl$

$= \frac{22}{7} \times 7 \times 25 = 550 \text{ m}^2$

Therefore, required length of cloth = curved surface area of tent/ width of cloth = 550/5 = 110 m

44. (B) Let Amal have = ₹ x and Sahaj have = ₹ y

According to question

$2(x - 30) = y + 30$

$2x - y = 90$ ...(i)

$x + 10 = 3(y - 10)$

$x - 3y = -40$ ...(ii)

From (i) and (ii)

$x = 62, y = 34$

Amal has = ₹ 62 and Sahaj has = ₹ 34

45. (C) Total score of all students

= 10 × 75 + 12 × 60 + 8 × 40 + 3 × 30

= 750 + 720 + 320 + 90

= 1880

Total number of students

= 10 + 12 + 8 + 3 = 33

Mean score =1880/33 = 57 (approx.)

46. (C) ΔABC is rightangled triangle with AB = AC and AD is the bisector of ∠A.

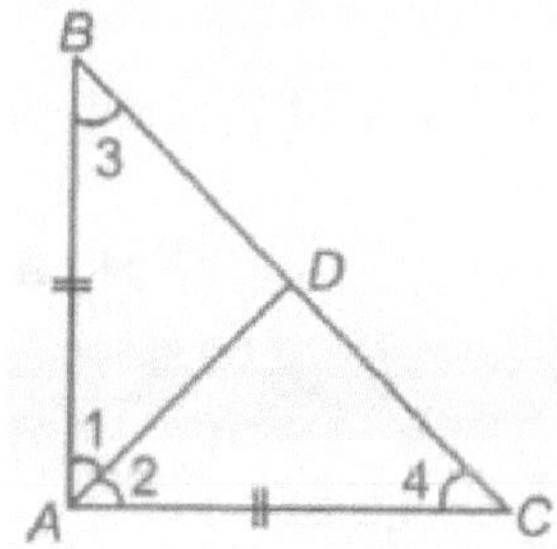

∠B = ∠C [angles opposites to equal sides are equal]....(i)

Now, in $\Delta ABC, \angle A = 90°$

and $\angle A + \angle B + \angle C = 180°$

$\Rightarrow 90° + \angle B + \angle B = 180°$

[From (i)]

$\Rightarrow 2\angle B = 90° \Rightarrow \angle B = 45°$

$\Rightarrow \angle B = \angle C = 45°$ or $\angle 3 = \angle 4 = 45°$

Also, $\angle 1 = \angle 2 = 45°$

[$\because$ AD is bisector of $\angle A$]

Also, $\angle 1 = \angle 3, \angle 2 = \angle 4 = 45°$

$\Rightarrow BD = AD,\ DC = AD$ ...(ii)

[Sides opposite to equal angles are equal]

Thus, $BC = BD + DC = AD + AD$

[From (ii)]

$\Rightarrow BC = 2AD$

47. (A) In the given figure
$y + 55° = 180°$ [Co-interior angles]
$y = 125°$
$x = y = 125°$ [Corresponding angles]
$z + 55° = 90°$ [Interior angles]
$z = 35°$

48. (C) Volume of each cube = 125 cm^3
No. of cubes in the given figure = 15
Thus, volume of the structure
= 15 × 125 = 1875 cm^3

49. (C) Alternate interior angles = ∠3 = ∠5
Co-interior angles = ∠3 = ∠6 = 180°
Corresponding angles = ∠2 = ∠6
Vertically opposite angles = ∠2 = ∠4

50. (B) Area of canvas lost in wastage = 1 m^2
Now, surface area of tent = 550 m^2

$\pi rl = 550$

$\frac{22}{7} \times 7 \times l = 550$

$l = 3\frac{550}{22}\text{ m} = 25\text{ m}$

$l^2 = r^2 + h^2$

$h = \sqrt{l^2 - r^2} = \sqrt{25^2 - 7^2}\text{m}$

$= \sqrt{625 - 49}\text{ m} = 24\text{ m}$

Volume of the conical tent

$= \frac{1}{3}\pi r^2 h = \frac{1}{3} \times \frac{22}{7} \times 7 \times 7 \times 24\text{ m}^3$

$= 1232\text{ m}^3$

NATIONAL SCIENCE OLYMPIAD (NSO)

MOCK TEST PAPER – 1

ANSWERS

1. (B)	2. (D)	3. (A)	4. (A)	5. (C)	6. (D)	7. (B)	8. (A)	9. (C)	10. (D)
11. (A)	12. (A)	13. (C)	14. (D)	15. (B)	16. (B)	17. (C)	18. (B)	19. (D)	20. (A)
21. (D)	22. (C)	23. (C)	24. (B)	25. (A)	26. (A)	27. (D)	28. (A)	29. (C)	30. (A)
31. (B)	32. (C)	33. (D)	34. (A)	35. (A)	36. (A)	37. (C)	38. (A)	39. (D)	40. (C)
41. (B)	42. (D)	43. (A)	44. (C)	45. (A)	46. (A)	47. (A)	48. (C)	49. (A)	50. (D)

6. (D) X was multiplied with 3 to obtain Y. All are correct except 56×3 = 168

7. (B) G B C D E F A
Alphabets represent the initials of the names.

8. (A)

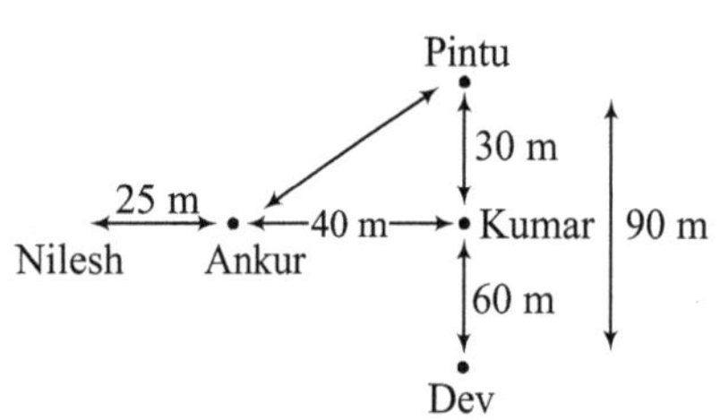

9. (C) Let your friend's age today = X years
After two years age will be (X+2) years.
Hence,
X + 2 = 2 (X–8) ↔ X + 2 = 2X–16 ↔ X = 18 Years

10. (D) The digits connected through the line are square or square root of each other.

13. (C) Camphor can be separated by sublimation.

14. (D) The gas with lowest boiling point is highly volatile, so it will be distilled out first. The gas with highest boiling point

is least volatile, so it will be distilled out last.

16. (B) Mass of ammonia = 8 g
Molar mass of ammonia = 17 g/mol
No. of moles of ammonia = 8/17 mol
Let's assume the mass of SO_2 = X

$$\text{Amount of } SO_2 = \frac{\text{Mass of } SO_2}{\text{Molar mass of } SO_2} = \frac{X}{64}\text{mol}$$

For equal number of molecules, the number of moles should be same.

$$\frac{X}{64} = \frac{8}{17}$$

$$X = \frac{8 \times 64}{17} = 30.1 \approx 30 \text{ g}$$

17. (C) P and Q possess same number of protons but vary in the number of neutrons i.e.; their atomic number is same, but their mass number is different, therefore P and Q are isotopes of each other. The chemical properties of isotopes are same, but their physical properties are different.

18. (B) Two atoms which have the same mass number, but their atomic numbers are different are termed as isobars of each other.

19. (D) Due to higher concentration outside of the cell, water starts moving out, it is called Exosmosis, due to exosmosis, the cell shrinks.

20.(A) A cell wall produces an opposite pressure on the cytoplasm, which results in the limitation of the exosmosis that eventually prevents cell-bursting.

21. (D) Only solvent molecules are allowed to pass through the semi permeable membrane.

23. (C) Muscles of heart are termed as cardiac muscles. They are uninucleate and branched.

24.(B) Bryophytes are also known as amphibians as they can grow on moist land but need water layer for reproduction.

25. (A) The cell wall is not found in animals, so it is not a criterion of classification of animals.

26. (A) Let, Mahira run with v speed for next 15 min.
Given, the average speed

$$= \frac{\text{Total distance covered}}{\text{Total time taken}}$$

$$\therefore 15 = \frac{\text{Total distance covered}}{\left(\frac{20+15}{60}\right)\text{hr}}$$

$$\text{Total distance} = 15 \times \frac{35}{60} = \frac{35}{4}$$
$$= 8.75 \text{ km}$$

Distance covered in 20 mins

$$= 18 \times \frac{20}{60} = 6 \text{ km}$$

Remaining distance = 8.75 – 6 = 2.75 km
Hence, for next 15 min

$$v = \frac{2.75}{\frac{15}{60}} = 2.75 \times 4 = 11 \text{ km/hr}$$

27. (D) Position and acceleration of B1 will be same as of B2.

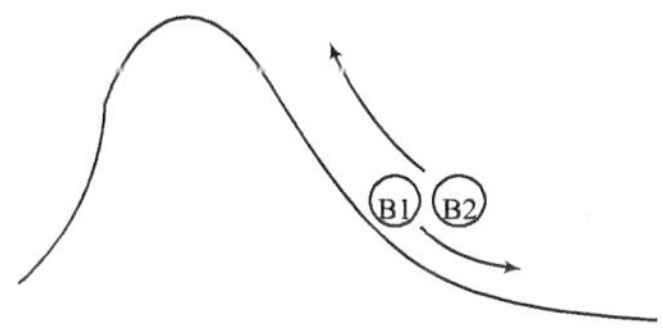

28.(A) As the velocity of the both moving bodies is same and brakes provided equal retardation therefore the distance of the both bodies will be same.

29. (C) Rate of burning of fuel $= \frac{dm}{dt} = 2$ kg/s

Velocity of fuel ejection = 30 km/s = 30000 m/s

$$\text{Thrust} = \frac{dm}{dt}.v = 1 \times 30000 = 30000 \text{ N}$$

Thus, the force exerted on the rocket = 30000 N.

32. (C) Frequency of the sound waves does not depend on the medium. It will be same in air and water.

33. (D) Amplitude of the sound wave = 1 m (as given)

Wavelength

$$\lambda = \frac{V_s}{\vartheta} ......(i)$$

In 120 sec, the number of oscillations = 480

In 1 sec, the number of oscillations = $\frac{480}{120} = 4$

Frequency of the sound wave = 4 Hz

Putting the value of in eq (i)

$$\lambda = \frac{V_s}{\vartheta} = \frac{348}{4} = 87 \text{ m}$$

34. (A) Reverberation refers to the continuous reflection of the sound in an enclosed room or body.

35. (A) Placenta provides nutrition to the foetus. Through placenta pathogens can also travel upto the foetus.

36. (A) R is a wrong statement because only female Anopheles carries the malarial pathogens.

37. (C) Viruses use the host's machinery to perform their several processes.

42. (D) Macronutrients are required by the plants in rich amount.

45. (A) Common carp is omnivorous therefore it feeds on the bottom.

47. (A) Molar mass of $Fe_2(SO_4)_3$ = 400 g

$$\text{No. of moles} = \frac{\text{given mass}}{\text{molar mass}} = \frac{80}{400} = 0.2$$

As we know, 1 mol of $Fe_2(SO_4)_3$ contains 2 moles of Fe, so, 0.2 mol of $Fe_2(SO_4)_3$ contains 2 × 0.2 = 0.4 mol of Fe.

As we know, 1 mol of $Fe_2(SO_4)_3$ contains 12 moles of O, so, 0.2 mol of $Fe_2(SO_4)_3$ contains 12 × 0.2 = 2.4 mol of O.

As we know, 1 mol of $Fe_2(SO_4)_3$ contains 3 moles of S, so, 0.2 mol of $Fe_2(SO_4)_3$ contains 3 × 0.2 = 0.6 mol of S.

48. (C) Ratio of C, H, N = 12: 2.5 : 14, the whole number ratio = 24: 5: 28

As we know,

$$\text{Atomic Ratio} = \frac{\text{Ratio}}{\text{Atomic mass}}$$

Atomic ratio of C = $\frac{24}{12} = 2$

Atomic ration of H = $\frac{5}{1} = 5$

Atomic ratio of N = $\frac{42}{14} = 3$

Thus, empirical formula of the compound = $C_2H_5N_3$

Empirical mass of the compound =

$$n = \frac{\text{Molecular mass}}{\text{Empirical formula mass}} = \frac{243}{81} = 3$$

Molecular formula = n × empirical formula

= 3 × $C_2H_5N_3$

= $C_6H1_5N_9$

50. (D) Bryophytes are non-vascular plants, e.g., liverworts. Pteridophytes are vascular plants but are seedless, e.g.; equisetum, Gymnosperms are naked seeds bearing plants e.g.; pines, angiosperms are highly evolved seed coat bearing plants, e.g.; ipomoea.

MOCK TEST PAPER – 2

ANSWERS									
1. (C)	2. (D)	3. (D)	4. (A)	5. (B)	6. (A)	7. (C)	8. (D)	9. (D)	10. (C)
11. (C)	12. (D)	13. (D)	14. (B)	15. (A)	16. (D)	17. (C)	18. (C)	19. (A)	20. (D)
21. (B)	22. (C)	23. (B)	24. (C)	25. (A)	26. (A)	27. (C)	28. (A)	29. (D)	30. (A)
31. (B)	32. (B)	33. (C)	34. (D)	35. (A)	36. (D)	37. (B)	38. (C)	39. (C)	40. (C)
41. (B)	42. (B)	43. (D)	44. (A)	45. (D)	46. (A)	47. (C)	48. (D)	49. (B)	50. (C)

8. (D)

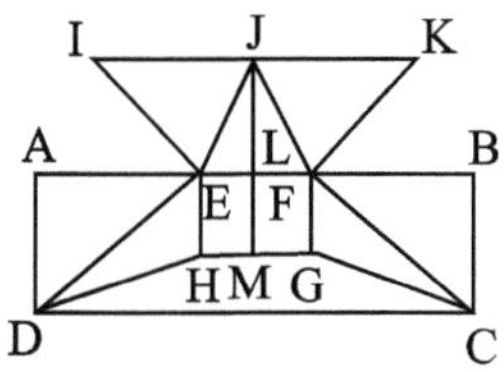

9. (D) In a true dice the sum of numbers of two opposite faces equals to 7. So on opposite of 5, the number would be 2.

11. (C) Micronutrients are those essential nutrients which are required by the plants in a very low amount.

13. (D) X, Y and Z are drone, queen bee and worker bee respectively. Parthenogenesis gives rise to drone while fertilized eggs develop into worker and queen bee.

14. (B) Process P is performed by plants, Q is performed by animals.

15. (A) CFC harms the ozone layer.

16. (D) The fertilizers used in the fields ultimately goes to water bodies which causes extensive growth of the algae as the fertilizers are rich in such nutrient which are required for the growth of the algae.

17. (C) Except dengue all are sexually transmitted diseases. Dengue is transmitted through a vector.

18. (C) Vaccines provide temporary active immunity against a particular pathogen.

21. (B) Speed of sound v = 320 m/s and frequency of sound υ = 640 Hz

$$\lambda = \frac{V_s}{\upsilon} = \frac{320}{640} = \frac{1}{2} = 0.5 \text{ m}$$

22. (C) Soft objects absorb some of the sound energy.

24. (C) mass m = 40 kg
Height of the staircase (h)

$$h = 130 \times \frac{20}{100} = 26 \text{ m}$$

$$\text{t} - 100 \text{ s}$$

$$\text{P} = \frac{\text{mgh}}{\text{t}}$$

$$= \frac{40 \times 10 \times 26}{100} = 104\text{W}$$

25. (A) Height = h, time = T/10 s
As we know

$$\text{s} = \text{ut} + \frac{1}{2}\text{at}^2$$

$$\therefore \text{ h}' = \frac{1}{2}\text{g}\left(\frac{\text{T}}{10}\right)^2 \qquad (\text{as u} = 0)$$

$$\text{so, h}' = \frac{1}{2}\text{g}\frac{\text{T}^2}{100} = \frac{1}{100}\left(\frac{1}{2}g\text{T}^2\right) = \frac{1}{100}\text{h}$$

So, the position of the ball above the ground

$$\text{h} - \text{h}' = \text{h} - \frac{\text{h}}{100} = \frac{99\text{h}}{100}m$$

26. (A) For a freely falling object the acceleration due to gravity is always directed downwards.

28. (A) If all the balances are equal to zero, only then a ball can move with steady speed.

29. (D) h = 30 m

$v^2 = u^2 + 2gh$; $v^2 = 2gh$ (as u= 0)

Ball bounces at the height h'= 15 m

So, $0^2 = v'^2 - 2gh'$

Acceleration of the ball

$$a = \frac{\sqrt{2 \times 9.8 \times 15} + \sqrt{2 \times 9.8 \times 30}}{0.1}$$

$$= \frac{41.40}{0.1} = 414 \text{ m/s}^2$$

31. (B) The flowers are generally pentamerous and the leaves show reticulate venation. Tap root system is commonly found in dicots.

32. (B) Crocodiles possess all the characteristics given in the passage.

33. (C) The label 'a' refers to the dendrites, 'b' is neurilemma, 'c' is node of Ranvier and 'd' is the axon ending. The dendrites receive impulses while axon takes impulse away from the cell body or cyton.

36. (D) The secretion and transport of material to and fro of the cell is controlled by Golgi body, so it is also termed as the traffic police of the cell.

37. (B) Stroma is the site of dark reaction while granum is the site of light reaction.

38. (C) Electrons revolve and have fixed energy in a particular orbit.

41. (B) Atomicity of oxygen

$$= \frac{\text{Molecular mass of ozone}}{\text{Atomic mass of oxygen}} = \frac{48}{16} = 3$$

42. (B) On heating with sulphur, iron filings produce iron sulphide which is new compound. Its properties are totally different from iron filing and sulphur and both reactants can not be separated by normal physical methods.

43. (D) With the mixing of impurities the melting point of the substance decreases.

44. (A) Sublimation refers to the direct conversion of solid into gas without undergoing liquid state.

45. (D) The melting point is -30°C and boiling point is 70°C, it means between these temperature S is found in liquid state. Therefore it is liquid at 0°C as well. Below –30°C it is solid; hence it is solid at 100°C and above 70°C it is gas.

47. (C) P: Time taken between successive claps

$$= \frac{1}{20} = 0.05 \text{ s}$$

Q: Since one echo is heard, so the time taken between the last clap and its echo

$$= \frac{1}{20} = 0.05 \text{ s}$$

$$\text{Distance} = 330 \times \frac{1}{20} \times \frac{1}{2} = 8.25 \text{m}$$

48. (D) Endothermic reactions use energy, exothermic reactions release energy. Latent heat refers to the heat required to convert a solid into a liquid or vapour, or a liquid into a vapour, without change of temperature.

50. (C) Archimedes' principle of buoyant force (F_B) suggests that,

F_B = Volume of the object immersed in the liquid × density of the liquid × acceleration due to gravity

Let volume of the object = V

For water,

$$F_B = \frac{2V}{3} \times \rho_w \times g = \frac{2V}{3} \times \rho_w \times 10 = \frac{20V}{3}\rho_w \quad \text{......(i)}$$

For alcohol,

$$F_B = \frac{1V}{5} \times \rho_a \times g = \frac{1V}{5} \times \rho_a \times 10 = 2V\rho_w \quad \text{.......(ii)}$$

From both equations;

$$\frac{20V}{3}\rho_w = 2V\rho_a$$

$$\therefore \frac{\rho_a}{\rho_w} = \frac{20}{6} = \frac{10}{3} = 3.33$$

NATIONAL CYBER OLYMPIAD – NCO

MOCK TEST PAPER – 1

ANSWERS									
1. (D)	2. (B)	3. (B)	4. (A)	5. (B)	6. (C)	7. (D)	8. (B)	9. (D)	10. (C)
11. (C)	12. (D)	13. (A)	14. (C)	15. (B)	16. (C)	17. (A)	18. (D)	19. (B)	20. (C)
21. (A)	22. (D)	23. (B)	24. (C)	25. (A)	26. (A)	27. (C)	28. (D)	29. (B)	30. (C)
31. (C)	32. (D)	33. (C)	34. (C)	35. (B)	36. (A)	37. (C)	38. (A)	39. (B)	40. (D)
41. (A)	42. (C)	43. (B)	44. (B)	45. (C)	46. (C)	47. (A)	48. (A)	49. (B)	50. (C)

1. (D) In the other alternatives, three letters are in lowercase.

2. (B) YOU = 25 + 15 − 21 = 19, and YUP = 25 + 21 − 16 = 30. So, MEN = 13 + 5−14 =4

3. (B) C%D means D is C's wife. D+E means D is sister of E. E F means E is father of F. So, the F is son of bother of C's wife. Therefore, F is either niece or nephew of C.

4. (A) Step IV: is injurious to health consuming. Step V: alcohol is injurious to health. Step IV: Consuming alcohol is injurious to. In this arrangement he is keeping the previous word and deleting the last word.

5. (B) The number of only Hindi and English language speaking people are 2500 + 7500 + 9000 = 19000.

6. (C) The distance of the women from her initial position is 2 (cos45°) × 9 = 14.14 m.

7. (D) The terms that were followed by a letter, but not preceded by a numeral are: 6, C, D, 3, 8, $, @, 3.

8. (B) The complete series is:

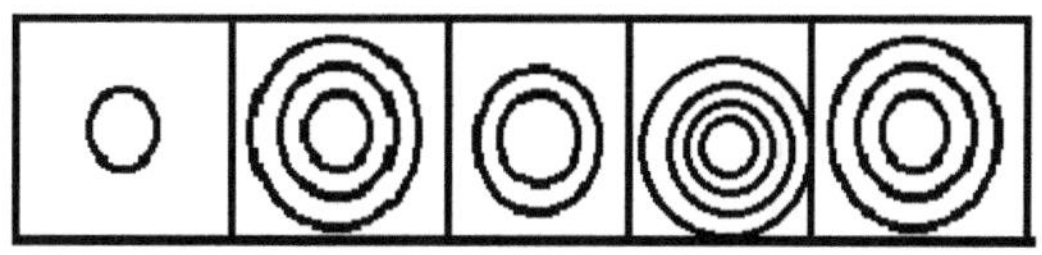

9. (D) The numbers of triangles in the given figure is 12.

10. (C) The water image of the given figure is

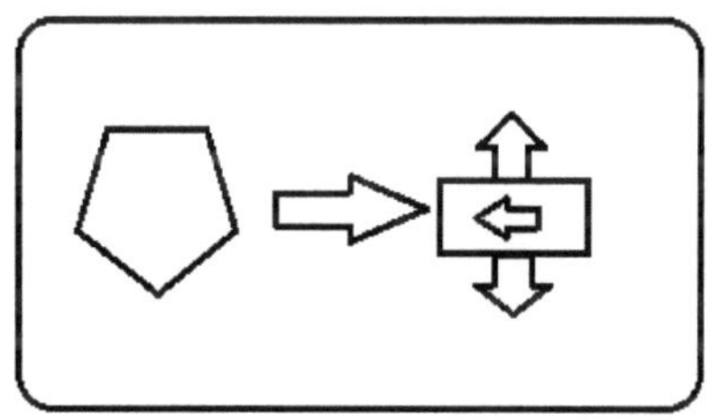

11. (C) The code "<target>" defines where to open the link document.

12. (D) The tags <cr> and </cr> are used to add rows into a table.

13. (A) void, hsides and box are valid values of frame attribute, but around is not.

14. (C) The shortcut key "Ctrl + W" is used to close document.

15. (B) The AutoRecover feature saves information after specified minutes.

16. (C) Page Width.

17. (A) The given shortcut key applies the outline border to selected cells.

18. (D) The shown icon is used to remove arrows drawn by both Trace Precedents and Dependents.

19. (B) The Evaluate formula allows a user to debug a formula by executing each part of the formula individually.

20. (C) The trigger icon is .

21. (A) The shortcut key used for changing the font size is Ctrl + Shift + P.

22. (D) Compare.

23. (B) Malware.

24. (C) Virtual Private Network

25. (A) SSL technology is used to create a secure and private connection between two or more computers.

26. (A) The purpose of DSL is to transfer digital signals over standard telephone lines.

27. (C) The time taken to pass a message from one node of network to other is called as latency.

28. (D) Repeater.

29. (B) Google Goggles.

30. (C) Head Mounted Display

31. (C) A CMOS can maintain its configuration setting due to the battery present on mother board. So, the user needs to replace the CMOS battery.

32. (D) Among the given types, USB is not an internal type hard drive.

33. (C) The credit/debit cards uses magnetic type storage technology to store data.

34. (C) The loop structure is used to allow an operation to be repeated for fixed number of times.

35. (B) The instruction in algorithm are written from top to bottom.

36. (A) 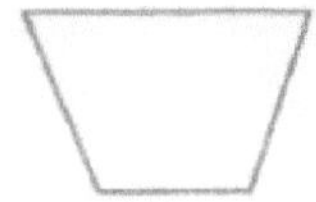

37. (C) The method to stopping of an animated character for a specific number of frames is called as freezing.

38. (A) Musical Instrument Digital Identifier.

39. (B) Linear

40. (D) Graphic

41. (A) Erasing tool is used to slow in or slow out the speed of an object in animation.

42. (C) The shown tool is known as free transform.

43. (B) Integrated development environment.

44. (B) Interaction mode is not a valid mode of Visual Basic application.

45. (C) The INCORRECT match is Text box – .

46. (C) The figure shown is categorised as color and IK bones tools.

47. (A) The output of the given HTML code is 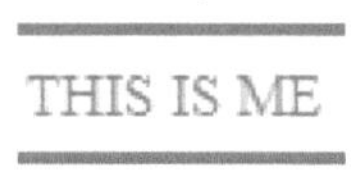

.

48. (A) a-(iii), b-(iv), c-(ii), d-(i)

49. (B) A software is said to be robust if it can cope up data errors.

50. (C) For input output statements, parallelogram shape is used.

MOCK TEST PAPER – 2

ANSWERS

1. (A)	2. (C)	3. (A)	4. (C)	5. (D)	6. (A)	7. (B)	8. (A)	9. (D)	10. (D)
11. (B)	12. (D)	13. (B)	14. (D)	15. (A)	16. (C)	17. (C)	18. (D)	19. (D)	20. (C)
21. (B)	22. (B)	23. (A)	24. (D)	25. (C)	26. (B)	27. (A)	28. (D)	29. (B)	30. (A)
31. (C)	32. (D)	33. (B)	34. (A)	35. (B)	36. (D)	37. (C)	38. (A)	39. (D)	40. (B)
41. (D)	42. (C)	43. (C)	44. (B)	45. (A)	46. (A)	47. (C)	48. (D)	49. (B)	50. (A)

1. (A) The pattern is +2, −-4. So, the complete series is − 2, 0, − 4, − 2, − 6, − 4, − 8…

2. (C) The pattern for the coding is −1, + 2, + 1, + 1, + 2, -1. So, 'CHROME' is written as 'BJSPOD' in that code.

3. (A) The son of the her only daughter-in-law is the grandchild of women. If the man is grandfather of son of her only daughter-in-law, then the man is her husband.

4. (C) Among them, only B is good in singing, dancing and badminton.

5. (D)

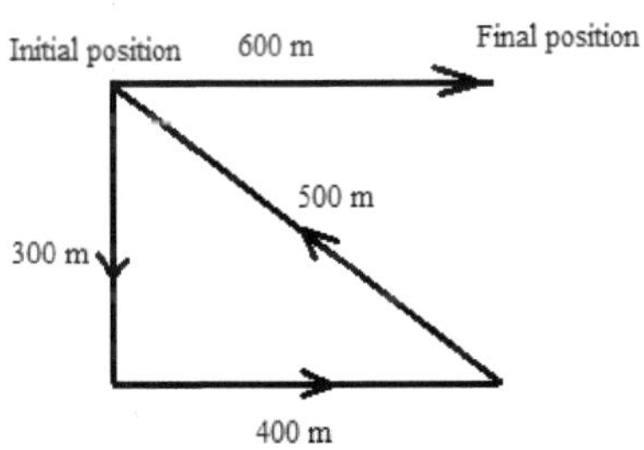

6. (A) The arrangement of the given word in a dictionary would be: Assertion, Assume, Assumption, Assure (That is 3, 1, 4, 2)

7. (B) The mathematical expression for given relation is: 6 × 5 + 4 – 4 × 2 % 4 = 32

8. (A) The complete series is:

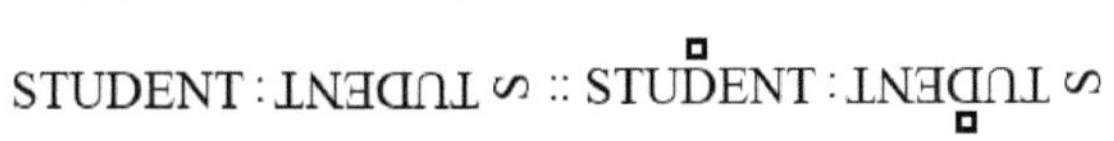

9. (D) The mirror image of the given combination is

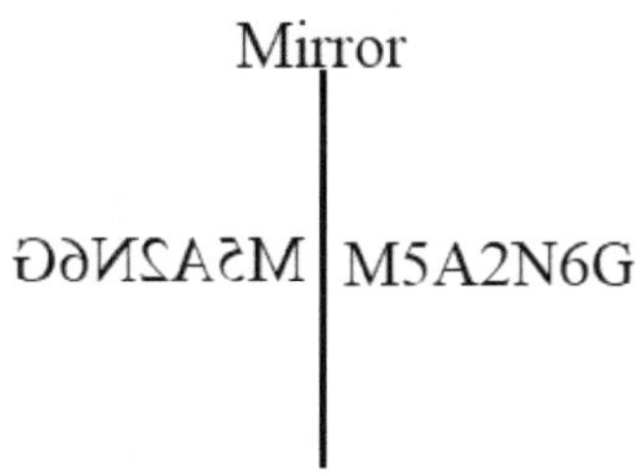

10. (D) The best alternatives that represents the folded sheet is:

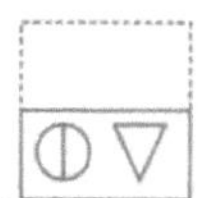

11. (B) The graphical user interface enables a user to click and drag objects with mouse instead of entering commands.

12. (D) The 'SDIO' enables devices to use SD slot to support Bluetooth adapters, GPS receivers. It can also be used for interface of input or output devices. But, they are non-volatile type memory card.

13. (B) The flash CS6 is a type of multimedia software.

14. (D) The statements which sets or resets the value stored in a variable are called assignment statements.

15. (A) The shown figure is an example of decision symbol flowchart.

16. (C) An algorithm is a self contained step-by-step set of operations to be performed in the given sequence.

17. (C) Morphing.
18. (D) Equalizers.
19. (D) Non-Linear media allows users to go forward or backward while playing a movie through DVD.
20. (C) 24
21. (B) Gradient Transform
22. (B) All of the given options are filter types, excluding gradient shadow.
23. (A) var = 3 – 2 Mod 1 + 1 – 2 = 3 – 0 + 1 – 2 = 2.
24. (D) Function key 'F9' is used to insert or toggles a breakpoint in visual basic.
25. (C) The shown tool is known as frame.
26. (B) The Cellpadding attribute is used to control the space between a cell's border and its contents.
27. (A) The user is trying to change the text color to black.
28. (D) The tag used to add cells in a row of a table is <td>.
29. (B) The key "Ctrl + Alt + C" is used to insert copyright symbol.
30. (A) Reviewing Pane.
31. (C) Navigation Pane.
32. (D) The shown icon is used to view the document in full screen mode.
33. (B) The shortcut key for AutoSum function of MS Excel 2010 is Alt + =.
34. (A) Using of COUNTA function will return the number of non-blank cells in a range.
35. (B) The shown icon is for Object.
36. (D) The correct match from the option is Hyper link – .
37. (C) The shortcut key to switch between Slides and Outline pane in Normal View is Ctrl + Shift + Tab.
38. (A) Wireless Local Area Network.
39. (D) The device connects your computer to your phone line and provide access to the network is modem.
40. (B) Antivirus.
41. (D) Patch Cable.
42. (C) Pixar Animation Studios.
43. (C) FireWire.
44. (B) Switches give better network performance than hubs.
45. (A) Wikipedia.
46. (A) Replace.
47. (C) The symbol 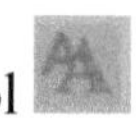 is used change the set of styles, colors and fonts used in the document.
48. (D) Consolidate
49. (B) Network hub conserves network bandwidth while delivering the message.
50. (A) a-(iii), b-(iv), c-(ii), d-(i)

MOCK TEST PAPER – 1

ANSWERS

1. (C)	2. (D)	3. (A)	4. (B)	5. (C)	6. (A)	7. (B)	8. (B)	9. (B)	10. (C)
11. (C)	12. (A)	13. (B)	14. (B)	15. (B)	16. (D)	17. (B)	18. (D)	19. (A)	20. (B)
21. (B)	22. (C)	23. (C)	24. (C)	25. (A)	26. (D)	27. (B)	28. (B)	29. (C)	30. (B)
31. (A)	32. (B)	33. (C)	34. (B)	35. (A)	36. (A)	37. (B)	38. (B)	39. (B)	40. (C)
41. (C)	42. (B)	43. (B)	44. (D)	45. (C)	46. (B)	47. (B)	48. (A)	49. (C)	50. (C)

1. (C) Discrimination

2. (D) All of these

3. (A) Someone whose job is to travel with musicians and move their equipment.

4. (B) Two birds with one stone

15. (B) A question mark is used to end an interrogative sentence.

23. (C) In the sentence subject includes 'I' and the friends, hence there are more than one people.

28. (B) Duplicate does not belong to the category of the other words. All the words except duplicate are synonyms to each other.

30. (B) Except 'Moral' all are synonyms of notorious.

MOCK TEST PAPER – 2

ANSWERS

1. (D)	2. (B)	3. (D)	4. (C)	5. (C)	6. (A)	7. (B)	8. (B)	9. (D)	10. (C)
11. (A)	12. (A)	13. (B)	14. (C)	15. (C)	16. (A)	17. (B)	18. (C)	19. (C)	20. (B)
21. (B)	22. (C)	23. (B)	24. (A)	25. (C)	26. (A)	27. (C)	28. (B)	29. (A)	30. (A)
31. (A)	32. (C)	33. (A)	34. (C)	35. (B)	36. (A)	37. (C)	38. (C)	39. (B)	40. (A)
41. (C)	42. (B)	43. (C)	44. (C)	45. (C)	46. (B)	47. (B)	48. (C)	49. (B)	50. (B)

4. (C) All are synonyms of each other except domestic and familiar.

6. (A) This proverb can be understood with another proverb, 'the thread usually breaks at its thinnest point.'

8. (B) Collective noun stand for a group of people or something.

9. (D) Jay and Veeru are two persons.

11. (A) Downstairs is the adverb of the place.

20. (B) To not feel well

24. (A) Concord refers to the grammatical agreement between two parts of a sentence.

29. (A) An exclamation mark is used after an imperative sentence if the command is urgent and forceful.

35. (B) Abandon means to give up completely.

9 789357 942348

Printed by Libri Plureos GmbH in Hamburg,
Germany